Three Propositions

Eleven Other Essays

Three Propositions

&

Eleven Other Essays
(1953-1969)

by

Neville Goddard

Contents

Three Propositions

Well, my first proposition is this one. The individual state of consciousness determines the conditions and the circumstances of his life. The second proposition is that man can select the state of consciousness with which he desires to be identified; and the third follows naturally--therefore, man can be what he wants to be.

If the first proposition is true that the individual's state of consciousness is the sole cause of the phenomena of his life, then the normal, natural question that is asked "Why doesn't he change it to a more desirable state if he could change it?" Well, that is not as easy as it appears.

Today we hope to give you a technique to make it easier but man finds it very hard to leave the things to which he has grown accustomed. We are all grown stuck in the habitual. It may seem strange but a very sordid cartoon appeared years ago, that is during the last war; you might have seen it, it came out in the "New Yorker" and it was one by George Price. In it is one single little room, a sink piled high with unwashed dishes, plaster falling from the walls, and these two middle-aged people, she sitting on a chair reading a letter, disheveled, matted hair, and he with torn clothes and feet stuck upon the table and socks exposing holes, and the caption of the picture is this. She is reading a letter from her soldier son abroad: "He says he's homesick." Now you should see the interior of this house--one room, completely disheveled-but the lad was homesick!

Now man finds it difficult to detach himself from the habitual; so this morning we have brought you these three propositions, and I hope I can make it clear that you can with this knowledge apply it so that you can realize your every objective. It is the height of folly to expect changes to come about by the mere passage of time, for that which requires a state of consciousness to produce its effect could not be effective without such a state of consciousness. So if I must be in the consciousness of the thing that I am seeking before I find it, then the only thing to do is to acquire that state of consciousness. Most of us do not even know what we mean by state of consciousness. To those who are here for the first time it is simply meant by state of consciousness the sum total of all that a man believes and accepts and consents to as true.

Now it need not be true; it may be, but it need not be true, it could be false, it could be a half truth, it could be a lie, it could be a superstition, it could be a prejudice, but the sum total of all that a man believes constitutes his state of consciousness. It is the house in which he abides, and as long as he remains in that house similar problems will confront him, the circumstances of life will remain the same. He may move physically across the ends of the earth but he will encounter similar conditions; he can't get away from the house in which he abides. The Bible speaks of these houses as mansions of the Lord, it speaks of them as cities, it speaks of them as rooms, as upper rooms, all kinds of words are used to describe individual states of awareness. And the appeal in the Bible is always to move out and occupy the upper story, meaning to move up to a higher level within one's self.

Now, if you do not know the state in which you abide, it's a very simple technique you may employ to discover that state: for the man dwelling in a state, and we all dwell in states, could easily discover the state by listening within himself and observing his own internal mental conversations, for the state is singing its own song and it reveals itself in man's inner speech. If you will listen attentively and uncritically to what inwardly you are saying, you will discover the state. And it will not surprise you that things are as they are for you will hear within yourself the cause of the phenomena of life. So that what you are inwardly saying and doing is far more important than what you outwardly know or seemingly outwardly express; so when a man knows what inwardly he is doing then he can change it. If you have never uncritically observed your reactions to life; if you are totally unaware of your subjective behavior, then you are unaware of the cause of the things in your world. But if you become aware of the state, then you simply go about changing it.

Now here is a technique I have found most helpful and I find that it works like a miracle; anyone can do it. I know that some of you here possibly come from extreme orthodox walks of life and it may seem strange to you even to be here, but I assure you you are not alone, many of your leaders in the orthodox field seek an audience with the speaker; many a rabbi has been in my home, many a priest, and many a Protestant leader. Many of them. They come to my home for interpretations of the book that publicly they wouldn't dare give any interpretation other than the most extreme literal interpretation. So don't be surprised if you hear things here that might startle you; your leaders are startled; but this is a technique I have found most helpful.

First of all, man stands forever in the presence of an infinite and eternal energy, from which energy all things proceed but it follows definite patterns: it just doesn't move out of man and crystallize in things in some strange haphazard manner. It follows a definite track and the track it follows is laid down by the man himself in his own internal conversations. So though man is called upon to change his thinking that he may change his world, for we are told "Be ye transformed by the renewal of your mind", man can't change his thinking unless he changes his ideas for he thinks from his ideas. So if I would change and become transformed, I must lay new tracks and the tracks I lay are always laid down in my own internal conversation. So what am I saying now when seemingly I am alone? I can sit in that chair, or stand here, or walk the streets and I can't stop talking. Man does not realize that he is talking, because he is never still enough to listen to the voice speaking within himself, but inwardly he is whispering what outwardly is taking place as conditions and circumstances.

Most of the things he whispers are negative in justifying his behavior. There is no need to justify. He is excusing delay or excusing failure, or he is arguing, or he is judging harshly or he is condemning. Many of us have secret affection for hurts: we don't want to be liked by certain people; we just wouldn't like it if they liked us. We just don't want certain things to take place in our world even though they may bring a greater comfort and a greater satisfaction. Man has a peculiar, strange feeling, a little affection for the feeling of being unwanted or the feeling of being hurt, and he likes to talk about it. Well, try to pull that man out of that habitual state: it would be just as difficult as to keep that soldier boy away from that sordid room; he goes back into the sordid rooms within himself. You don't see dishes unwashed within yourself, but if you could only see the internal psychological state in which most of us abide, we would see a room far dirtier than the one that George Price illustrated in the "New Yorker" magazine. They are all unwashed plates within us: on the outside we wash them but we are told in the Bible, we leave the inside unwashed and we become whited sepulchers.

Now, if I sincerely desire to change my world there is no one in my world I need change but myself, so that I don't need to change you as an individual but I do need to change my attitude towards you. If you dislike me or if I think you dislike me, or if your behavior offends me, the cause of my offense is not in you and your behavior but I must look for that cause within myself. Now if I seriously and I am honest about my search, I will find it and I will find that inwardly when I think of you it is never a pleasant conversation that I carry on with you. So let me sit down now and bring you before my mind's eye, and as I bring you before the mind's eye let me imagine a conversation which would imply a radical change in my world; let me bring you up and change my attitude toward you by laying new tracks relative to you.

These tracks will then become the tracks across which this eternal energy will pour, an energy which is only thinking; moving across the tracks laid down in my own inner conversations will result in changes in my outer world. Now, if I repeat the conversations and do it more often, then it becomes a habit and I will find that when I am about my Father's business in the outer world I am inwardly through habit carrying on these changed and lovelier conversations. Now, a transformation of consciousness will definitely result in a change of environment and conditions. But I mean transformation of consciousness, I do not mean a slight alteration of consciousness like a change of mood.

It is nice to change a mood from some unlovely to a lovely, but I want a transformation and by transformation I mean that when one state into which I have moved and move so often that it becomes a habit and that state grows stable, so that it expels from my consciousness all of its rivals, then that central habitual state defines my character and really constitutes my new world. It spells out a transformation, but if I only do it a little bit and return to my former state, then I might have had a temporary lift but I will not notice radical changes in my outer world. I will notice these changes in my outer world if inwardly I have truly changed. Then without effort on my part I will find the outer world changing to correspond to the changes that took place within me.

So you bear it in mind, I can't stress it too often, I can't give it too great importance, this wonderful thing called man's ability to talk within himself and without the aid of anyone in the world, sitting alone at home you can construct a sentence which would imply the fulfillment of the ideal; you can construct a sentence which would imply that a friend I blessed that she has realized her objective, that the thing you know she wants she has. So what would she say to you had she realized it? Well, you listen attentively as though you heard and you will really hear if you are still enough you will hear as coming from without what really you are whispering from within yourself.

Man is this wonderful temple in which all the work takes place and the outer world is only a projection of the work done within himself. This, called present man, unfortunately is asleep. It is told us so beautifully in the Bible that Adam slept, in the second chapter of Genesis. He was placed into a profound sleep from which he has not been awakened. There is no reference in the Bible where Adam was ever awakened from his sleep but there is a reference where he awoke but not as Adam; he awoke as a second man called Christ Jesus. So in Christ they awake: in Adam all sleep, but a man who is totally unaware of the mental activity that goes on within him is the one who sleeps as Adam: he doesn't know it. He walks with his eyes wide open, he may be a very important person in the world, he may be wealthy, he may be famous, he may have all the things that you admire, but if he is totally unaware of that mental activity which is the cause of the phenomena of his life, that man is sound asleep and he is personified as Adam.

And he will read his Bible and think it is a literal story; he will read where Adam was put to sleep and from Adam a rib was taken and a woman was formed called Eve, but when a man begins to awake he realizes that this symbolical Eve of the Bible is only his own emanation now called by the name of nature. And nature is his slave, and must fashion life about him as he fashions it within himself. But if he is asleep, he fashions it in confusion, but he fashions it anyway, for he uses the very technique that his Father used to build a world. He uses speech, he uses inner talking, and that's how this whole vast world was brought into being; so he uses the same technique, he has speech and he has mind, but in the state of sleep he brings about strange conditions, and he doesn't know he's the cause of the strange things round about him. As he begins to awake, then he awakes only as one being, he awakes as Christ Jesus and the being called Christ Jesus personified in our Gospels is simply the awakened, loving imagination.

Imaginative love where only love guides it is incapable of hearing anything but the lovely. When that being begins to awake he doesn't see things in pure objectivity, he sees everything subjectively related to himself. He is incapable of meeting a stranger; he may meet one for the first time but he knows it is not really a stranger, that the man had no power to come into his world save he from within himself drew him. "No man comes unto me save I call him;" "No man takes away my life, I lay it down myself": "You didn't choose me, I have chosen you". Though you seemingly come now for the first moment in my life, you still didn't choose me, I have chosen you. I see then every being subjectively related to myself. So in that state you become incapable of hurt, you've overcome all the violence that formerly you've expressed in the world when you were asleep. There is no condemnation to the sleeping man, he is dreaming confusion because he doesn't know who he is: but he begins to awake by such techniques as given you this morning.

If you take this technique and you try it consciously, for here I am appealing not to the passive mind that passively surrenders to appearances, I am appealing to the Christ in you which is the active conscious use of your lovely imagination. So when you sit down and you predetermine what you want to hear and you listen until you hear it, and you refuse to hear anything other than that, then you are using the one power in the world that awakens a man and you are using your lovely imagination, which is "Christ in you, the hope of glory."

Here is a lady this past week; she has heard the story of revision; her husband calls her and it's a big deal, it runs into a fortune, he had sent off

600 feet of film to Acme and they've returned the film, only the first 300 were good. The second three were duds, as they call it, not a thing was on it, a complete blank. Yet they were up against time, that 600 feet of film had to be on a plane headed for Chicago in the immediate present, less than twelve hours away, it had to be there, that was the contract, and 300 feet of film taken, no sound appeared, with the whole thing a blank.

She sat down when her husband called her, desperately called her: she sat on the bed just where she had received the call, put the receiver up, and sat in the silence until she heard within herself that phone ringing and across that wire the same voice, but now not an anxious voice but a tender loving voice, which was her husband, explaining that the whole thing had been resolved, they had found what seemingly they had lost forever. She sat in the silence for one hour and ten minutes, and there she listened and she listened until her whole body became still in hearing only what she wanted to hear. And an hour and ten minutes later while still in the silence the phone rang; it's her husband calling to say that Acme just called him to explain and excuse themselves, it was their mistake, they had found the missing 300 feet of film. And there was not a dud, it wasn't a blank, the whole thing was perfect.

Now the average person, not knowing this law of revision or even those knowing it, would have accepted as final the evidence of sense and receiving news that seemed so factual they would have gone into a stew, bawled out Acme and pulled all kinds of wires to correct it. But she heard and she acted upon it, and that's what I mean when I tell you that a little knowledge if you carry it out in action will be far more profitable than much knowledge which you neglect to carry out in action; now many of you present and this is no judgment, you have the same knowledge that this lady has; she's been coming here recently but she heard, she attended all the meetings at the Ebell, and she's been here; undoubtedly she's here this morning, but at least she came the first two Sundays and she hasn't missed one at the Ebell, and having heard the art of revision, she acted upon it.

Others heard the art of revision: have you acted upon it? Did you last night allow the sun to descend upon your wrath? Did you sleep last night with any trouble, any vexation unresolved? Or did you last night truly go to bed having resolved every vexation and trouble of the day? All the little problems, each one must be resolved, you rewrite the play. If you didn't rewrite yesterday's events and make them conform to the ideal you wish you had experienced, then you heard but you aren't a doer. And so you are told in the Bible, "Would that ye be doers of the word and not mere hearers only." For if you are a hearer and not a doer, then you are like a man who sees his face in the glass and turns and straightway forgets what manner of man he is. But if you are a doer and not a forgetful hearer, then you shall be blessed with the deed, for you will look into the law of liberty and you will liberate yourself and liberating yourself you shall be blessed with the deed.

For those of you who are Bible students and want to check it, read the Book of James. You will find that story in the first chapter of the Epistle of James, where he looks in and liberates himself--well she liberated herself by listening until she heard exactly what she wanted to hear, and she heard it one hour and ten minutes later. Now the majority of people I say they would not have acted upon it: through habit they would have gone into a stew; they would have fumed and fretted, and that very day had he brought home the negative news that undoubtedly he would have, they both would have slept allowing the sun to descend upon their wrath.

But now you know that there's not a thing on the outside to change, that first proposition is true, that the man's state of consciousness, which simply means all that he accepts, all that he believes, all that he consents to, that and that alone is the cause of the phenomena of his life. Man can change his state of consciousness and therefore man can determine the conditions of his life. But the passage of time will not in itself do anything; time is only a facility for changes in experience but it cannot produce the change. It is simply that which allows changes to take place, but it can't produce them. Space gives us the facility for experience and time for changes in experience, but of themselves they do nothing. We must operate the power, and so the individual if he doesn't become the operator then he will wait in vain.

So no one here this morning, in fact no one coming here through the year should ever allow himself to blame another, ever allow himself to justify failure, for he is only betraying his own lack of the use of this law. Anyone that you listen to who is complaining of a third party, he has no idea how he is betraying himself, he is telling you of his own unwashed dishes within himself, but he doesn't know it. He thinks it is in the one that he is now judging, but as he talks to you listen attentively and see what must be washed within him and you aid him. In your own mind's eye rewrite that script that you heard and when you leave him just imagine you heard a more lovely conversation than the one you did hear. Just rewrite it for him and in some strange way lift him up within you, for that's your task; it's my task.

We aren't here to condemn, we are here to redeem; having awakened we have found Christ in us as our own imagination and so our duty, as it is said Christ's duty is to do the will of him that sent me and the will of him that sent me is that "Of all that he has given me I should lose nothing", but I shall raise it up again and I raise it up by encountering someone and then finding him down I raise him up 'within myself '. I simply hear what I want to hear from him. Now my voice you are hearing this morning, you could take the tone, listen attentively and you will hear this tone within you; when you hear the tone within you, then put upon that tone the word that you want to hear and having put it upon it, listen and do not move until you hear this tone conveying these words. But make them noble; don't take that tone and put upon it any word outside of the word which would imply a dignified, noble state, because you are not hurting anyone but self. If you take someone and you put words upon that tone or that voice, and the words do not imply a noble spirit, then you are only allowing that being to be down within you, you are not really performing your duty.

So here this morning, believe these propositions and then having believed them, do something about it. Go out and take what we have told you concerning inner speech: it is truly the greatest of the arts. You listen and only hear what you want to hear. You take your imaginary hand and put it into the hand of a friend, the imaginary hand of a friend, and there you congratulate him on his good fortune. If you want one to congratulate you, you allow yourself to be congratulated. You don't bend the head, you hold it high and accept the congratulation, and when you congratulate him imagine that he is fully conscious of the good that is already his and he accepts that congratulation and make the contact real.

That is truly entering the kingdom of heaven, for you enter the kingdom and the kingdom is within you, it's not without, and you always enter the kingdom by a loving, knowing communion. You can enter the kingdom at every moment of time, ride the street car, ride the busses, and with all the talking and gossiping, you can enter the kingdom and bless a friend by just imagining the friend is with you and you are putting your hand into his and congratulating him on the good news you've heard concerning him, and listen as though he answered in kind, and in that moment you have actually blessed him. He may be a thousand miles away but from that moment on things begin to stir within his world for you have brought about a change within the structure of his mind and every modification of the structure of a man's mind must result in corresponding outer changes.

So you bring about these lovely changes within you. Look at the testimonial--one you heard this morning; here is a pile of letters and this is really a tight, tight pile. It is one of the biggest piles I think that you have received here and this week's mail I can't begin to tell you what a thrill it is to receive, one after the other not begging for help any more but giving praise and thanks for the principle that brought the help into their world. I can't tell you how many in the last two weeks have received an increase in income, increase of position, a better state of health; things happened because they did something about it. They were not just warming a seat here on Sunday morning and waiting for things to happen by association: they produced the thing by producing it first within themselves.

So here this appeals to men who are big enough to stand on their own feet: men who want spiritual meat and who have outgrown the milk given to sleeping man. So if you want the literal concept, you are still asleep and this really would not be the place to get it, for from this platform you are going to be given meat, spiritual meat, for you must go out and do something about it. If you have the greatest knowledge in the world concerning foods and you didn't eat, you would die of starvation, and so it's not the knowledge of it, it's the application of it that counts.

Now this coming week, we start tomorrow, and it's an interesting one for those who like their Bible, those who would like to put their mental teeth into it tonight and come tomorrow night with some intuitive knowledge of it, it's the 49th chapter of Genesis; you'll find many of them I'll quote tomorrow, but in the 49th of Genesis here is what it says. First of all he calls his sons together to tell them their future and there are twelve of them. It's Jacob calling his sons, but the fifth one, when he calls the fifth one, he tells him the scepter shall never drop, shall never depart from your hand, never, not in eternity. His name is Judah, the one that fathered the line that flowered in Christ Jesus, when you read the genealogy as given to us in Matthew and Luke.

Then it said of Judah that he took his foal and he tied it to a vine and he took the colt of an ass and tied it to a good vine, and then he washed his garments in wine and he washed his clothes in the blood of grapes. And his eye was red with wine and his teeth white with milk. Well now, those of you who still would like to read that literally, you may get some satisfaction out of washing your clothes in wine--I don't, I'd rather drink it, but some wash theirs in the blood of grapes and then the teeth white with milk and the eye bloodshot with wine. Well now, that was the one who fathered out of Thamar the twins that brought forth the line that flowered in Christ Jesus. So go back and read the genealogy of Judah and then see what Judah did and how he took two animals, one was a foal and one was a colt.

Now I won't tell you the interpretation: you exercise your intuitive faculty and you come tomorrow night and you hear what we have to say about the amethyst, or the wine stone: how a man must make the amethyst, how a man must take his garments, a thing that clothes the mind of man and wash them in the blood of grapes, how a man not only must do it but his eye must become equally bloodshot with wine and his teeth white with milk. And we will show you tomorrow night why they placed upon him the scarlet robe and then placed upon him the most mystical of all--the purple robe; so as they placed them up to the very final act was the placing of the purple robe upon the man who had awakened, who is now ready to ascend on high, to higher levels within himself.

But you can't ascend until you first make the purple robe and although we have orders in this world who have scarlet robes and purple robes, no man can make it for you. And so it cannot be woven in any factory, it has to be woven from the factory within yourself. So tomorrow night for those who are vitally interested in going deeper into the mysteries our subject is "The Twelfth, an Amethyst". The very last act of a man, the twelfth, for there are only twelve, then comes the most, I would say, the least precious of all stones in the eyes of man, but in the eye of God it's the most precious and it's not the little thing you find among the stones, it's the one you find within yourself. So that is tomorrow's subject.

A Movement *of* Mind

In the 33rd chapter of the Book of Job we are told that God speaks to man in two ways, but man does not perceive them. It is said: "In a dream, in a vision of the night when deep sleep falls upon men while they slumber on their beds, he opens the ears of men and seals their instructions." Tell that to a psychiatrist and, because he separates the dreamer from God, he will tell you that all dreams come from the individual dreamer and not from God. But I tell you: God's eternal name is I AM, and if I asked who is dreaming the dream would the individual not say, "I am?" And are we not told that that is God's name forever and ever?

You cannot separate the dreamer from God, and all dreams proceed from Him. Some are simple and need no interpretation, while others are revealed in a symbolic language and need an interpreter, as told us in the story of Joseph. His true identity is revealed when he looked into the faces of those who had had a dream and saw they were disturbed, for he said: "Do not interpretations belong to God? Tell me your dream." Then he interpreted the dreams of the butler, the baker, and even Pharaoh himself, and they all came to pass just as he had said they would. Now, if only God can interpret a dream, why tell Joseph? Because he is a personification of God. His name was changed from Joseph (meaning "salvation") to Joshua, which means "Jehovah is salvation."

Now back in 1954, I awoke from a dream hearing these words: "You do not move in waking any more than you move on your bed in sleep. It is all a movement of mind. The intensity is determined by the strength of the vortex you create, which is just like a whirlwind with a center of perfect stillness. You only believe that you are moving when you are awake, as you think you move in sleep." Well, I am a rational being and reason could not accept that statement, but I wrote it down and placed it in my Bible to await further revelation.

Psychiatrists would say this message came from myself. I will not deny that, but I do know that it came from a depth of my own being which my rational mind does not reach. Today our three astronauts returned from a trip of half a million miles. You and I came here tonight in our cars, and throughout my lifetime I have traveled all over the world in ships and planes. And like Blake, in my dreams "I have traveled through a land of men, a land of men and women, too. And heard and seen such dreadful things as cold earth wanderers never knew." We have all traveled, yet I know what I heard and wrote down. I know that I have traveled in my dreams and yet I know I have not physically left my room, for when I awoke in the morning I was still on the bed upon which I fell asleep. So I ask you: is this waking state no more than a dream? Is there a dreamer in the depths of my being who looks upon this world as a dream, just as I who -having gone to a little lower of the dream at night -awake to find I haven't left my bed at dawn?

Paul tells us that "We are born anew through the resurrection of Jesus Christ from the dead." I remember that night, for I felt myself waking from a deep, deep sleep, feeling a vibration which, although centered in my head, it seemed to be coming from without. Then I awoke within the sepulcher -the skull -in which I was buried, to come out to find all of the symbolism of the Christian mystery surrounding me. I saw the infant wrapped in swaddling clothes and the three witnesses to the event. Although unseen, as I was spirit, the witnesses spoke of me as the father of the child -the sign that my savior was born, fulfilling scripture: "This shall be a sign unto you, you shall find a child wrapped in swaddling clothes, lying in a manger." That night I awoke from a far deeper level of my being to find the symbolism of my waking from the dream of life, just as day after day I wake from the dream of the night. So, could it be that the revelation I heard back in 1954 is literally true? Reason questions it, reason doubts it, and reason rejects it. So if the vision is true then reason is rejecting Jesus Christ, for Jesus Christ defines himself as the truth, saying: "I am the truth..." If the revelation is true, and reason rejects it, is not reason Satan, the doubting one?

This statement cannot be logically proved. Its truth must be experienced. I had completely forgotten it until I discovered my note today while looking in my Interpreter's Bible, and there it was -the note I wrote on the 28th day of November 1954: "You do not move in waking any more than you move on your bed in sleep. It is all a movement of mind. The intensity is determined by the strength of the vortex you create, which is just like a whirlwind with a center of perfect stillness. You only believe that you are moving when you are awake, as you think you move in sleep."

Scripture speaks of two ages: this age of darkness and decay, and that age of light and eternal life. This age is one of motion and violence, turbulence and storms, as the dreamer in men is sound asleep and does not know that he is God. In the 44th Psalm, however, he is urged to "Rouse thyself, why sleepest thou, O Lord. Awake! Do not cast us off forever." While occupying his dream God has the sensation of travel, motion and violence; but when he awakes he will find himself in the sepulcher, the skull of Man, where he deliberately laid himself down to sleep and was buried. God crucified himself on the cross of man and is dreaming this dream of life so that man may become God.

Now I want to clarify a few points. In the Book of John this statement is made: "His voice you have never heard, his form you have never seen, neither does his word abide in you because you do not believe him whom he has sent." Many of you have completely accepted the fact that I have been sent. You believe me when I tell you that I stood in the presence of the Risen Lord, who embraced me and I became one with. Having been incorporated into the body of Love, Almighty God sent me to tell my experience. Having accepted my words, many of you have had a sexual experience with me, in vision, and have interpreted this to be a physical experience on this level; but it is not, as this is a shadow world. Your acceptance brought about this union, yet I -the speaker -am totally unaware of it. The true story of Christ which I have brought you has now been made alive in you. It will erupt in time and your experience of scripture will be identical to mine.

The males who have completely accepted my words will not experience a sexual act, but an embrace. Wearing the body of the Risen Lord, who is Infinite Love and with whom I am now one, you will see my face. You will be asked to name the greatest thing in the world and, as though divinely inspired, you will quote the words of Paul saying: "Faith, hope, and love; these three, but the greatest of these is love." I will embrace you, and you will fuse with the one body of the Risen Lord, and he who is united with the Lord becomes one Spirit with him.

All of these are symbols, telling you that, having believed him whom he sent, you will hear his voice and see his form as his word is now abiding in you. It's a complete break with the past, as told us in the first words the Risen Lord spoke in the Book of Mark: "Repent and believe in the gospel." The gospel is the good news that man is not lost; that scripture is not secular history, but divine history, which was plotted and planned before we came out from the Father and came into the world to enter our own creation and play all the parts.

It is God who awakes in you. One man, containing all, fell into diversity as told us in the 82nd Psalm: "I say, 'You are gods, sons of the Most High, all of you; nevertheless, you shall die like men, and fall as one man, O princes.'" (I have quoted the Revised Standard Version in the marginal setup which is the true translation of the Hebrew.) It takes all the sons who fell, to form God the Father; so we are gathered together one by one into that same body which fell into humanity. And from humanity, God extracts himself individually because we are all so unique. No one can be duplicated or lost, because God is buried in all and God is redeeming himself.

Today I watched the exciting touchdown of the astronauts who had traveled to the moon and back. Then I reread what I had written back in 1954: "You do not move in waking any more than you do on your bed in sleep." Now, reason could not accept that statement. I saw the astronauts return. We have a record of their journey of a half-million miles, yet they did not move? Well, I must confess that I have traveled in my dreams, as I am sure you have; yet we always wake on our bed in the morning, do we not? Could there be a dreamer far deeper than the one who is dreaming this seeming waking state? And when he awakes from the dream of life, would he not look upon it as you look upon the dream of the night? I know that when I awoke from within, I realized that I had been there for unnumbered centuries, dreaming violence, love, hate, concupiscence, and pain -dreaming everything to be real, just as I did in any dream. I awoke to discover that I had been in that skull for centuries, dreaming I was a man walking the earth, dying, being restored to life to die again. This I continued to do until that moment in time when I awoke in Golgotha, the sepulcher where I was buried in the beginning of time. That's my Calvary.

I seem to move here. I get up and shave in the morning, bathe, eat, make an effort to earn a dollar to pay the rent, and do all sorts of things; yet it's all a dream, a dream with a purpose. God limited himself to the limit of contraction and opacity called man and began to dream this world into being. Now believing himself to be you, you can dream noble dreams or ignoble ones. I urge you to dream noble dreams, because when you know you are the dreamer you can make all of your dreams come true.

A dream is a very fluid state. Knowing what you want to dream, bring your inner circle of friends before your mind's eye and allow them to see you as you want to be seen. When you are self-persuaded this is now a fact, relax in the vision's gestation period. There is an interval of time between impregnation and birth. Having seen the expressions on their faces and heard the sound of their voices, break the spell and wait for that impregnation to take place in the world of dreams, while you live in the world of Caesar awaiting its coming.

I have told you that the story of Jesus Christ has unfolded itself within me. What I shared with you tonight is not recorded in scripture; but in the very last verse of the 21st chapter of John he makes this statement: "Many other things Jesus did which are not recorded here. Were every one of them to be written, the world itself could not contain the books." There was no need to record the words which were revealed to me; so it does fit in with the very last verse of the epilogue of John, for John ends on the 20th verse and the 21st is the epilogue. All of these things happened and many more, but only these were recorded that you may believe.

Thank you for sharing your visions with me, as they are showing me that you have completely accepted the story as I have told it. I have shared with you the true story of Jesus Christ. Over the centuries, barnacles have gathered around the ship. Men, in the interest of their own doctrines, have added to the scriptures. In spite of the warning not to add to or take from the words of the prophecies of the Bible, men have added to, to support their own traditions and conventions. When the original text was written, the one who had the vision simply recorded it. He did not understand it, but wrote it down, as I did, knowing that a greater revelation would come.

I could not understand what I heard in 1954; but in 1959 I knew its truth, for I awoke from a profound dream to discover that I was not on my bed, but in my skull and completely alone. I came out of my skull to find the babe wrapped in swaddling clothes and the witnesses to the event. Seeing the babe, they witnessed the sign of my spiritual birth, but they could not see me as having been born of the spirit. I am Spirit, while they, not yet born of the spirit, are flesh. I didn't bring forth a little baby; the child is but a sign that God is born. Having begotten himself, he brings forth that which he buried in humanity, for God is redeeming himself, as there is only God in the universe.

The Bible hasn't a thing to do with any morals as the pulpits teach. It makes no attempt to change the world, as it is a schoolhouse. You don't turn a schoolroom into a home. This is a school of educated darkness, where we travel towards the light. Scripture does not attempt to change things; rather it urges all to "Render unto Caesar the things that are Caesar's."

To try to make this world a nice, sweet little place in which all are happy and have enough to eat and drink is fine, but that hasn't a thing to do with the mystery of Christ. Were there no struggle, no effort would be made to awaken from the dream of life. Rather, the sleeper would fall deeper into sleep. So, let them march along telling the world how to become good and kind. It's all nonsense, for as long as man wears the garment of the animal he must express it. Taking from himself the heart and mind of Love, God took upon himself the body, heart, and mind of the animal, as told us in the 4th chapter of Daniel. This is an animal world, but while in this world of violence Jesus Christ awakes to discover it was only a dream. Were it not that Jesus Christ was in you, you could not breathe, for your very breath is his life.

The day will come when you will awake to know this to be true; for David, the sum total of all of the experiences you have had in your dream of being man, will stand before you and call you "Father". Then you will fulfill the 89th Psalm knowing, "I have found David. He has cried unto me, 'Thou art my Father, my God and the Rock of my salvation.' "Having played all the parts of Man, humanity, fused into a single youth, reveals your Godhood.

As the Father, you will know that your son has always done your will; for you will have found in David, the son of Jesse (I AM) one who has done all your will. You, the Father, dreamed it and you, the son. played all the parts. And when the play is over you awake to come out of Golgotha to be born from above. Peter tells us: "We are born anew through the resurrection of Jesus Christ from the dead." While the world worships him as someone coming from without, you will find him rising from within -not as another, but as your very Self, the dreamer of life.

The great poet, Shelley, saw it so clearly when he said: "He has awakened from the dream of life. 'Tis we who, lost in stormy visions, keep with phantoms an unprofitable strife." That's what the world is doing, fighting self-created phantoms. The world is yourself pushed out and you are in conflict with yourself until that day when an unearthly wind possesses you and you awake in your skull with the consuming desire to get out. With your innate knowledge, you will push the base of your skull and something will move. Then you will come out just as a child comes out of the womb of a woman; but this time you are being born, not from below, but from above -from the skull of Self. The word "anothin" is translated "from above." When Pilate said: "Do you not know that I have the power to crucify you or the power to set you free," the Risen Lord replied: "You have no power over me unless it were given to you from above." Here is the same word "anothin." The power to kill or make alive comes from within.

Everything is taking place from within. Having fallen into a profound sleep, you are the Lord Jesus Christ, dreaming the dream of life. And because there is only one Being, everyone will awaken as Jesus, for everything else will vanish and leave Jesus only. And no one can say that Jesus is Lord except by the Holy Wind. When that wind possesses you, you awake within yourself. Only then will you know you are the Lord Jesus Christ.

Now let us go into the silence.

An Inner Conviction

I tell you that imagination creates reality and I ask you to imagine a state, any state, which would imply the fulfillment of your desire. It doesn't really matter what anyone else thinks; it's what you think that matters to you! If you create a scene which implies the fulfillment of your desire and dwell in it until you have an inner conviction that it is real, what does it matter what another thinks?

In the Book of Habakkuk (which means "to embrace") the prophet speaks to the Lord as: "Thou who art of purer eyes than to behold evil." Then he asks the question: "Why are you silent when the wicked swallows up the righteous? I will take my stand upon the watchtower, to see and hear what people say to me and what I will answer." Now the Lord speaks, saying: "Write the vision plain upon the tablets so that he who runs may read it. For the vision has its own appointed hour; it ripens and it will flower. If it be long, then wait, for it is sure and it will not be late."

There are those who try to rush everything into being. They try to force birth from conception, but it cannot be done. There are many experiences not recorded in scripture, and I am not here to stand in judgment of anyone as to whether they have experienced scripture or not. But I do know from experience that on this level, if you dare to assume you are what you want to be, your inner conviction, your feeling of certainty will bring it to pass. When you embrace the desired state, you have assumed its impregnation, and its fulfillment has its own appointed hour. It will ripen and flower. If the state is slow in objectifying itself wait, for it is sure and will not be late.

I know that when I was told I could not get out of the island of Barbados for at least six months and I desired to leave immediately, I assumed I was walking up the gangplank of the ship. I felt the dampness of the rail and tasted the salt air of the sea with the feeling of certainty that I was leaving for America. I made that gangplank so real that I hadn't even broken the spell before the phone rang and I was offered passage for the following week. Although I had been told that I was on the bottom of a list of over two thousand names, my family and I were singled out to board that ship. So I know that the truth of any concept is known by the feeling of a certainty, a peculiar knowingness that it is true.

You can take this same concept into all levels of your being, for any desire is a concept. You can move into any desire and express it. Ask no one if you are entitled to it or if you did it -only you know what you did. It happened to you. Now wait for the vision (the desire's fulfillment) for it has its own appointed hour. It ripens, it will flower. If it seems long then wait, for it is sure and it will not be late.

Returning to the overall picture of God's rising in Man, let us go back to the Book of Exodus, where we are told: "The time that the people of Israel dwelt in Egypt was four hundred and thirty years. And at the end of four hundred and thirty years, on that very day all the hosts of the Lord departed from Egypt. It was a night of watching by the Lord." Then Moses is told to keep this night in memory.

Scripture teaches a mystery. "Great indeed is the mystery of our religion." The word "mystery" is defined as "a religious truth revealed by God that man cannot by reason alone discover." Here is a doctrine of revealed truth.

We are told in the 15th chapter of Genesis that "You and your descendants will be enslaved for four hundred years." Now, the number four hundred is the twenty-second letter of the Hebrew alphabet whose symbol is the cross. Your body (of beliefs) is the cross referred to as four hundred, and as long as you wear it you are enslaved in a land that is not yours. But in the end you will be brought out with great possessions!

In the 12th chapter of Exodus, thirty years has been added to the four hundred, and in the New Testament it is said that Jesus began his ministry when he was about thirty years of age. In this world you are enslaved, and here you remain playing your part until you are embraced, impregnated, and thirty years later Christ is born in you and your trials and tribulations are over! So four hundred does not mean years, but thirty does. Four hundred records the length which Blake calls 6,000 or 8,500 years. Call it what you will, it is the period of time man plays his part in this world. Then comes the moment when, as Man, you are selected, called and embraced, and told to stand upon your watch; for the sign has its own appointed time to ripen and to flower, and that time is thirty years!

My friend, Benny, does not remember the embrace, but I remember it well. It was in 1929. I was fully aware of the embrace, just as I was fully aware of its fulfillment in 1959, so I can tell anyone from my own experience how it happens, but I can't tell you when if you cannot remember the embrace. Only after impregnation can I prophesy as to what, and when these things will come into being.

But I do know that God's law reflects all the way down to this world of Caesar. I do not know how long it takes for each egg to hatch in a nest, but I do know each one will hatch in its own time. And so it is with an assumption. If I desire to be wealthy, I may not know how long it will take me to reach the conviction that I possess great wealth, but when I feel wealth is mine I have conceived. Conception is my end. The length of time between my desire and its conception depends entirely upon my inner conviction that it is done. A horse takes twelve months, a cow nine months, a chicken twenty-one days, so there are intervals of time; but it comes down to the simple fact that the truth concerning every concept is known by the feeling of its certainty. When you know it, not a thing can disturb your knowingness!

In my own case, as I felt the gangplank under my feet and the salt mist on the rail of the ship in Barbados, the phone rang and passage was mine. There have been other times when it has taken longer. Unfortunately we do not keep an account to see how long it takes to come about after we have done it. But a concept is an egg and remains so until occupied. Occupy your desire! Feel its certainty and you can prophesy its fulfillment.

Although I did not know what would become of it, I kept a record of what happened to me in 1929, so when I was born from above and raised from within myself in 1959, I looked back to discover that it was thirty years. I discovered that Jesus began his ministry when he was thirty years of age, and that Israel made their exodus thirty years after the four hundred recorded in Genesis. We are going to celebrate this exodus in the immediate future as the Passover, "a day to keep in memory forever." For "this is a night of watching by the Lord. On this day the Lord will bring the entire host of Israel out of the land of Egypt" and they will come out one by one. So if someone tells me a story that is not part of my experience, I cannot confirm it or deny it; I only know that my experiences parallel scripture.

But I say to you: everything has its own appointed time. It ripens and will flower. If fulfillment seems long, wait, for it is sure and will not be late. Everything comes on time, but we do not know the time interval because we do not record the conception. In my case, I keep a diary. I check scripture to find out where the passage is that I have experienced and record the date beside it. Now I know the length of time it takes to fulfill scripture. I also know that when it comes to the world of Caesar, I have received confirmation while in the silence. I have exploded right into the now and, having felt the thrill I knew it had to happen, but I did not know when. It could be a day, a week, or a month. Three weeks ago I heard good news for a friend, and today I received confirmation that it was completed. I will not catalog that event to say that particular desire equals all desires, because a desire can be as different as a chicken's egg is from the egg of an elephant. I do know, however that events of scripture do have definite time periods. Scripture fulfills itself in God's time, and you cannot delay it or hasten its coming.

A friend wrote me this week, saying: "I found myself sitting at a table looking at a beautiful plate containing a raw steak, when I heard the words, 'Eat it'. Obeying the command I then heard voice say, 'You have eaten the body of God.'" This lady has fulfilled the 51st to 56th verses of the 6th chapter of the Book of John: "My flesh is the bread of life. He who eats thereof has eternal life." She has completely eaten the body of revealed truth and eternal life is now hers. I cannot tell her when she will be called, but she has accepted the revealed truth, which is the body of God.

Another letter came, telling of how this lady spent the day working on her husband's books. She was so very tired that as she fell asleep, she said: "Father, I cannot take every aspect of the day and change it, but I can imagine that it never happened." So she began to create a scene which would imply that all the problems of the day were resolved, when out of the nowhere she saw an enormous scene of mountains clothed with magnificent trees. As she watched, she discovered that her mental activity caused the trees to move. And that the world pictured on the outside adjusted itself to be in harmony with her thoughts. Then she said "I came to the conclusion that my God is a God of action, for I saw everything I was imagining taking place now. I feel as though the world is moving in me like being on parade." That's how God sees Man. We are forever adjusting to his perfect being. He is looking out, yet everything is taking place within.

Tonight I ask you to take the most fantastic thing in this world and find an inner conviction within yourself that it is yours, for the truth of any concept is known by the feeling of certainty which that conviction inspires. Once you have that inner feeling of certainty, don't ask me to confirm it. What would it matter what I think? Do not be disillusioned if your experience has not been mine. Believe in yourself and trust your inner feeling. Test yourself and if it works on this level it will work in the depths of your being.

If, in my imagination I climb a gangplank, and as I look with nostalgia at the little island of Barbados and the phone rings, offering me the passage I desire, am I not influencing my outer world? Was the phone call not reflecting my mental activity? I arrived at the point of feeling a peculiar certainty, and that certainty was its inspiration.

You can always tell the truth of any concept by the feeling of certainty which it inspires. When you imagine seeing the world as you desire it to be and are inspired as to its truth, it doesn't matter what anyone else thinks. I don't care what it is; when you know what you want, you can make your desire so real, so natural that you will reach a feeling of certainty which no power in the world can stop. When that feeling is yours, drop it. Don't ask anyone if what you did was right or wrong; you did it and that's all that is necessary.

Now let me share the letter I received from Benny. He said: "Friends of mine (Negroes), a man and his wife, invited me to a party. On the way we stopped at their home, where a group of Caucasians in their teens were having a party. Suddenly my friends appeared in the doorway, coat and hat in hand, and said, 'You stay and mind the children.' I was shocked, but turned to look at the boys and girls, when out of the nowhere a blond, blue-eyed, fair skinned lad came toward me, and as I looked at him I knew he was David. He looked me in the eye and said, 'I know that our Father will never leave us.' At that moment I knew my son David, yet I also knew I fathered them all. This was on Wednesday. The following Friday as I told this experience to my friends, I awoke to discover that I had been dreaming, for I awoke on my bed."

Here is the doubling of a dream, the confirmation as told us in the 41st chapter of Genesis. Now, you cannot violate the story of scripture. David is described in the 16th chapter of 1 Samuel, and you will not change this description no matter who you are. The Christ child is not described, for he can be black, pink, white, or yellow. There is no description of Jesus either, but I will tell you who he is. He is the Ancient of Days as described in the Books of Daniel and Revelation. When you see David, he is the youth of the ancient one he observes. Benny is now wearing a very dark skin, but in the eyes of his fair skinned, blond and blue-eyed son David, Benny is the Ancient of Days, the Holy One of Israel. The one we recognize and call Benny now knows himself to be the Risen Lord. Now I will tell him that on the 8th day of July he will be split in two from top to bottom. I know, for the vision has its own appointed hour, it ripens, it will flower. If it seems long, wait, for it is sure and will not be late.

Now the Book of Ezekiel begins: "In the thirtieth year the heavens opened and I saw visions of God." Ezekiel gives you a day and a month, meaning nothing. The important thing is that in the 30th year the heavens opened and visions of God were his. "And as I looked, behold, a stormy wind." That's exactly what happens. An unearthly wind comes in that thirtieth year, and you are born from above, born anew through the resurrection of Jesus Christ from the dead. Jesus Christ is God's pattern of salvation buried in you. His death in the most literal sense is your life, and his resurrection is possible only after he impregnates himself.

God the sender and Man the sent are one. Falling in love with the one he sent, God impregnates him. He plants his seed, which takes thirty years to germinate and [is] his mission to start. This experience comes to Man after he has borne his cross in this wilderness world for thousands of years. In spite of the horrible things that take place in the world, when the individual is called and embraced, what does it matter what he has to go through before he awakens? In a short period of only 30 years he will be born into an entirely different age, for during that time he is taken out of this age and placed in that age, the age of the kingdom of heaven.

Now, because you know this concept, don't feel that you are better than someone else, you are creative power. Stand upon your tower and watch to see what God will say and how you will answer. Do this by assuming you are the person you want to be and seeing what you would see if your assumption was real. Remain there until you feel its certainty, until you reach the point of satisfaction, until you are convinced of its truth; and although the world may collapse around you, you will become that which you have assumed you are.

In the 21st chapter of the Book of John it is said that if all things were told concerning Jesus Christ, the world itself could not contain the books; so do not think that because I have not had your experience, that it is not true -but do not try to force me into accepting it. Believe what you choose and go your way this night. My pattern has followed scripture completely, from the embrace to the descent of the dove, but I am not saying it is the only way.

I am saying, however, that you can be the man (or woman) you want to be, but not by simply wishing. You must make the effort to look at the world mentally and see it reflect your fulfilled desire. And when it does you must remain in that state until you reach the inner conviction that what you are seeing, touching, tasting, smelling, and hearing is true, clothe yourself in the feeling of its reality -and explode! Do that and you are pregnant. And what do you do after pregnancy? Nothing! You simply wait for its birth to appear in its own appointed hour. And it will! When you least expect it your desire will objectify itself in the world for you to enjoy, whether it be health, wealth, or fame. That's how God's law works.

Now, to the one who had this experience the other night, I know you are anxious to give it birth right away, but what is thirty years in this fabulous eternity? You were awake when it happened, and you will never lose its memory. Should you depart tonight to find yourself a young lady of twenty, you would only be fifty when you brought forth the Christ child. Then you would see the complete pattern fulfill itself in three and a half years and enter a new age, which is the world of eternity. My dear, you are destined to know departure from this world of death and entrance into the world of eternal life as you move from darkness into light. But your reaction was natural.

It reminded me of a story I heard in New York City. This young girl came rushing into the subway, and standing in front of a gentleman she said: "Would you please let a pregnant lady have your seat?" Jumping up, terribly disturbed, the gentleman said: "When is the baby expected?" And she replied: "I don't know, it just happened." But this lady knows it will be thirty years, but what is thirty years when you have been called, you have been selected, you have been chosen. You are one of the elect!

Now let us go into the silence.

Believe It In

The objective reality of this world is solely produced by the human imagination, in which all things exist. Tonight I hope to show you how to subjectively appropriate that which already exists in you, and turn it into an objective fact. Your life is nothing more than the out picturing of your imaginal activity, for your imagination fulfills itself in what your life becomes.

The last year that Robert Frost was with us, he was interviewed by Life Magazine and said: "Our founding fathers did not believe in the future, they believed it in." This is true. Having broken with England, our founding fathers could have established their own royalty here by making one of them the king, thereby perpetuating a royal family. They could have chosen a form of dictatorship, but they agreed to imagine a form of government that had not been tried since the days of the Greeks. Democracy is the most difficult form of government in the world, yet our founding fathers agreed to believe it in. They knew it would take place, because they knew the power of belief -the power I hope to show you that you are, tonight.

To say: "I am going to be rich," will not make it happen; you must believe riches in by claiming within yourself: "I am rich." You must believe in the present tense, because the active, creative power that you are, is God. He is your awareness, and God alone acts and is. His name forever and ever is "I am" therefore, he can't say: "I will be rich" or "I was rich" but "I am rich!" Claim what you want to be aware of here and now, and although your reasonable mind denies it and your senses deny it -if you will assume it, with feeling, your inward activity, established and perpetuated, will objectify itself in the outside world -which is nothing more than your imaginal activity, objectified. To attempt to change the circumstances of your life before you change its imaginal activity, is to labor in vain. This I know from experience. I had a friend who hated Roosevelt, yet wanted him to change. Every morning while shaving, my friend would tell Roosevelt off. He found great joy and satisfaction in this daily routine, yet could not understand why Roosevelt stayed the same. But I tell you, if you want someone to change, you must change your imaginal activity, for it is the one and only cause of your life. And you can believe anything in if you will not accept the facts your senses dictate; for nothing is impossible to imagine, and imagining -persisted in and believed -will create its own reality.

Now, all things exist in God, and he exists in you and you exist in him. Your eternal body is the human imagination, and that is God Himself. Your imagination is an actual body in which everything is contained. When you imagine, the thing itself comes out of that divine body, Jehovah. The story of Jesus is a wonderful mystery that cannot be solved until you discover, from experience, that he is your own wonderful human imagination.

We are told that God speaks to man in a dream and unveils himself in a vision. Now, vision is a waking dream like this room, while a dream occurs when you are not fully awake. A few years ago this vision was mine: I was taken in spirit into one of the early mansions on 5th Avenue in New York City at the turn of the century. As I entered, I saw that three generations were present and I heard the eldest man telling the others of their grandfather's secret. These are his words: "Grandfather used to say, while standing on an empty lot: `I remember when this was an empty lot.' Then he would paint a word picture of what he wanted to build there. He saw it vividly in his mind's eye as he spoke, and in time it was established. He went through life in that manner, objectively realizing what he had first subjectively claimed."

I tell you: everything in your outer world was first subjectively appropriated, I don't care what it is. Desire can be your empty lot where you may stand, remembering when that which you now have, was only a desire. If I now say: "I remember when I lectured at the Woman's Club in Los Angeles" I am implying I am no longer there, and am where I want to be. Remembering when you were poor, I have taken you out of poverty and placed you in comfort. I remember when you were sick, by taking you out of sickness and placing you in the state of health. I remember when you were unknown, implies you are now known. By changing my memory image of you, I can now remember when you, with all your fame and fortune, were unknown and broke. That was the secret of grandfather's success.

This is what I learned in vision. Do not put this thought aside because it came to me in vision. In the 12th chapter of the Book of Numbers it is said that God speaks to man through the medium of dreams and makes himself known through vision. If God makes himself known to you through vision, and speaks to you in dream, what is more important than to remember your dreams and visions? You can't compare the morning's paper or any book you may read, to your vision of the night, for that is an instruction from the depth of yourself.

God in you speaks to you in a dream, as he did to me when he took me on a trip in time to that beautifully staffed mansion at the turn of the century. As spirit, I was invisible to those present; but I heard more distinctly than they, and comprehended the words more graphically then they, because they had their millions; and who is going to tell one who already has millions how to get them. I entered their environment to hear their story, in order to share it with those who will hear and believe my words and then try it.

This doesn't mean that, just because you heard my vision you are going to enjoy wealth; you must apply what you heard, and remember when. If you would say: "I remember when I couldn't afford to spend $400 a month for rent," you are implying you can well afford it now. The words: "I remember when it was a struggle to live on my monthly income," implies you have transcended that limitation. You can put yourself into any state by remembering when. You can remember when your friend expressed her desire to be married. By remembering when she was single, you are persuading yourself that your friend is no longer in that state, as you have moved her from one state into another.

When I say all things exist in the human imagination, I mean infinite states; for everything possible for you to experience now, exists in you as a state of which you are its operant power. Only you can make a state become alive. You must enter a state and animate it in order for it to out-picture itself in your world. You may then go back to sleep and think the objective fact is more real than its subjective state into which you have entered; but may I tell you: all states exist in the imagination. When a state is entered subjectively, it becomes objective in your vegetative world, where it will wax and wane and disappear; but its eternal form will remain forever and can be reanimated and brought back into being through the seed of contemplative thought. So I tell you: the most creative thing in you is to enter a state, and believe it into being.

Now, causation is the assemblage of mental states, which occurring creates that which the assemblage implies. Let us say that I have two friends who would empathize with me (not sympathize) if they heard my good news. I put them together and listen (all in my imagination) as they talk about me and what has happened in my life. Being true friends, I hear their words of joy and see their happiness reflected on their faces. Then I allow myself to become visible to them and feel their handshake and embrace as I accept their congratulations as a fact. Now I have assembled a mental state, which occurring, created that which the assemblage implied; therefore I am its cause. As I walk, firmly believing in the reality of what I have done, and that imaginal act becomes a fact, I may question myself as it how it came about. Then, remembering my imaginal act I would say: "I did it." If I did it, then did not God do it? Yes, because God and I are one "I am". Are you going to continue to believe there is another on the outside; or are you going to believe the great confession of faith, which I would urge you to accept? It's the great Sh'ma: "Hear O Israel, the Lord our God, the Lord is One." If the Lord is one he can't be two; therefore, if his name is I am and you say "1 am," you must be one with the Lord who brought the world into being.

Listen to these words: "By faith we understand that the world was created by the word of God, so that things that are seen were made out of things which do not appear." Here we see that the word of God is an imaginal activity, which -joined by faith -created the world. And faith is nothing more than the subjective appropriation of an objective hope. Now, when you discuss your desire with me, you cannot see my imaginal act relative to you. If you tell me you need a job and I accept that thought, when I think of you I remember your need. But if I changed your words and heard you tell me you loved your job, I could remember when you needed one; for now my memory bank contains the fact that you have a job you like very much. And when we meet again you tell me that you have it, you are only bringing confirmation of my imaginal, creative act.

Now, if imagination works this way, and it proves itself in the testing time and time again, what does it matter what the world thinks? It costs you nothing to try it, and what a change in life it will produce for you. Try it, for you will prove it in performance.

This may be in conflict with what you believe God to be. Maybe you still want him to be someone on the outside, so that there are two of you and not one. That's all right if you do, but I tell you: God became you that there would not be you and God. He became you, that you may become God. If God became you, his name must be in you, and it is; for if I ask you anything, you must first be aware of the question before you can respond, and your awareness is God.

You may not be aware of who you are, where you are, or what you are; but you do know that you are. Aware of what your senses and reason dictate, you may believe that you are limited, unwanted, ignored, and mistreated; and your world confirms your belief in your imaginal activity. And if you do not know that your awareness is causing this mistreatment, you will blame everyone but yourself; yet I tell you the only cause of the phenomena of life is an imaginal activity. There is no other cause.

If you believe in the horrors of the world as they are given to you in the paper and on television, your belief causes the horrors to continue. Believing the news of a shortage, you will buy what you do not need, blindly accepting the pressure to perpetuate an imaginal activity that keeps you frightened. All through scripture you are told to let not your heart be troubled, be not afraid, and fear not. If fear could be eliminated, there would be no need for psychologists or psychiatrists. It's a bunch of nonsense, anyway. Every day this branch of medicine changes their concepts and they are always in conflict as to what a man's attitude towards life is.

I say to everyone: the whole vast world is now in your human imagination, and you can bring any desire out of it by believing it into being.

First, you must know what you want, then create an image that fulfills it. Would your friends know and talk about it? Imagine they are with you now, discussing your fulfilled desire. You could be at a cocktail or dinner party that is being given in your honor. Or maybe it's a little get-together over tea. Create a scene in your mind's eye and believe its reality in! That invisible state will produce the objective state you desire, for all objective reality is solely produced by imagination.

The clothes you are now wearing were first imagined. The chair in which you are seated, the room that surrounds you -there isn't a thing here that wasn't first imagined; so you can see that imagining creates reality. If you don't believe it, you are lost in a world of confusion.

There is no fiction. What is fiction today will be a fact tomorrow. A book written as a fictional story today comes out of the imagination of the one who wrote it, and will become a fact in the tomorrows. If you have a good memory or a good research system, you could find today's facts. Not every fact is recorded, because not every thought is written; yet every person imagines. A man, feeling wrongfully imprisoned and desiring to get even, will disturb the world, because all things by a law divine in one another's being, mingle. You can't stop the force that comes from one who is imagining, because behind the mask he wears, you and he are one. Start now to become aware of what you are thinking, for as you think, you imagine. Only then can you steer a true course to your definite end. If you lose sight of that end, however, you can and will be moved by seeming others. But if you keep your mind centered in the awareness of dwelling in your destination, you cannot fail.

The end of your journey is where your journey begins. When you tell me what you want, do not try to tell me the means necessary to get it, because neither you nor I know them. Just tell me what you want that I may hear you tell me that you have it. If you try to tell me how your desire is going to be fulfilled, I must first rub that thought out before I can replace it with what you want to be. Man insists on talking about his problems. He seems to enjoy recounting them and cannot believe that all he needs to do is state his desire clearly. If you believe that imagination creates reality, you will never allow yourself to dwell on your problems, for you will realize that as you do you perpetuate them all the more.

So I tell you: the greatest thing you can do is to believe a thing into existence, just as our founding fathers did. They had no current example of democracy. It existed in Greece centuries ago, but failed because the Greeks changed their imaginal activity. We could do that too. Don't think for one second we have to continue as a democracy. We could be under dictatorship within twenty-four hours, for everything is possible. If you like democracy, you must be constantly watchful to keep its concepts alive within you. It's the most difficult form of government. A man can voice an opinion and stage a protest here, but in other forms of government he cannot. If you want to enjoy the freedom of a democracy, you must keep it alive by being aware of it.

Now, if you keep this law, you don't have to broadcast what you want; you simply assume that you have it, for -although your reasonable mind and outer senses deny it -if you persist in your assumption your desire will become your reality. There is no limit to your power of belief, and all things are possible to him who believes. Just imagine what an enormous power that is. You don't have to be nice, good, or wise, for anything is possible to you when you believe that what you are imagining is true. That is the way to success.

I believe any man who has been successful in his life's venture has lived as though he were successful. Living in that state, he can name those who aided him in achieving his success; and he may deny that he was always aware of success, but his awareness compelled the aid he received.

To believe your desire into being is to exercise the wonderful creative power that you are. We are told in the very first Psalm: "Blessed is the man who delights in the law of the Lord. In all that he does, he prospers." This law, as explained in the Sermon on the Mount, is psychological. "You have heard it said of old, thou shalt not commit adultery, but I say unto you, anyone who lusts after a woman has already committed the act of adultery with her in his heart." Here we discover that it is not enough to restrain the impulse on the outside. Adultery is committed the moment the desire is thought!

Knowing what you want, gear yourself towards it, for the act was committed in the wanting. Faith must now be added, for without faith it is impossible to please God. Can you imagine a state and feel that your imaginal act is now a fact? It costs you nothing to imagine; in fact you are imagining every moment in time, but not consciously. But, may I tell you: if you use your creative power by imagining a desire is already fulfilled, when you get it, the circumstances will seem so natural that it will be easy to deny your imagination had anything to do with it, and you could easily believe that it would have happened anyway. But if you do, you will have returned to sleep once again.

First of all, most of us do not even realize our own harvest when it confronts us. And if we do remember that we once imagined it, reason will tell us it would have happened anyway. Reason will remind you that you met a man (seemingly by accident) at a cocktail party who was interested in making money. When he heard your idea, he sent you to see his friend, and look what happened -so really, it would have happened anyway. Then, of course, it is easy to ignore the law, but "Blessed is the man who delights in the law of the Lord. In all that he does he prospers."

Don't forget the law while you are living in the world of Caesar, and apply it wisely; but remember you are not justified by its use. Justification comes through faith. You must have faith in the incredible story that God promised to bring himself out of you, as you! This is God's promise to all, and all are asked to believe it.

It is not what you are, but what you trust God to do, that saves you. And to the degree that you trust God to save you, you will be saved. But he has given us a psychological law to cushion the inevitable blows of life. The law is simple: "As you sow, so shall you reap." It is the law of like begets like. As you imagine, so shall your life become. Knowing what you want, assume the feeling that would be yours if you had it. Persist in that feeling, and in a way you do not know and could not devise, your desire will become a fact. Grandfather made his fortune by standing on an empty lot and saying to himself: "I remember when this was an empty lot." Then he would paint a beautiful word picture of the structure he desired there. This is a wonderful technique. You can remember when you were unknown, penniless, and ill, or a failure. Remembering when you were, implies you are no longer that, and your power is in its implication.

Use the law and it will take you from success to success, as you conceive success to be. As far as I am concerned, success is to fulfill the promise, and you cannot do that through the law. The promise is fulfilled through faith. Are you holding true to the faith? Examine yourself to see if you are. I have told you an eternal story. Believe it, but do not change it. The story is this: God became you that you may become God. Use the law to cushion the blows while God keeps his promise; and then one day, when your journey is over, you will say: "Into thy hands I commit my spirit. Thou hast redeemed me, O Lord, faithful God." That's the cry on the cross. Commit your spirit to your imaginal act, relax and fall asleep knowing its redemption is assured. Then when you least expect it, God will prove to you that he has redeemed you by awakening in you, as you. Then you will be born, not of blood or of the will of the flesh, or of the will of man, but of God.

Now let us go into the silence.

Imagination Creates Reality

Your own wonderful human imagination is the actual creative power of God within you. It is your savior. If you were thirsty, water would be your savior. If you needed a job, employment would be your savior. Your imagination is the power to save you from whatever circumstances you now find yourself. You can experience your heart's desire through the use of your imagination. Nothing is impossible to your imagination. Your imagination is unlimited in what it can accomplish. If you can imagine something, you can achieve it. Let me give you an example. If you were unable to walk and were confined to a wheelchair, you could close your eyes and imagine yourself running on the beach or wading in the water. If you would imagine yourself doing this until it took on the tones of reality, you could accomplish a healing that would allow you to actually walk or run.

The way to use your imagination creatively is this. Relax in a chair or on a bed and close your eyes. First determine what it is you wish to experience. Then, in this state of complete relaxation, bring to mind the end result of what it is you desire. In other words, if you were seeking a promotion at work, the end result might be that people would congratulate you on your promotion. You might move to a larger office. You would enjoy an increase in pay. Take any one of these events and, with your eyes closed, actually hear your friends congratulate you on your promotion. Feel their hand in yours as they tell you how happy they are for you. By actually feeling that you are being congratulated, your imagination will go to work to bring about that state in your outer world. You need not be concerned about how this will be accomplished. Your imagination will use whatever natural means are necessary to bring it about. "I am the beginning and the end." "My ways are past finding out." What you do in imagination is an instantaneous creative act. However, in this three-dimensional world, events appear in a time sequence. Therefore, it may take a short interval of time to realize in the outer world what you have just experienced in imagination. After you have performed this act in your imagination, open your eyes and go about your normal, natural affairs, confident that what you have done must come to fruition in your world. Make your inner conversations conform to your imaginal act. You have planted a seed and you will soon see the harvest of that which you have sowed.

When you go into your imagination, make sure that you are actually performing the action, hearing the words, touching the object, or smelling the aroma in your self- conceived drama. What you do in your imagination is not merely a daydream in which you see events in your mind's eye. You must enter the dream as if you were actually there. You must make "then" now and make "there" here. To make this perfectly clear, imagine that you would experience driving a new car after you have achieved your goal. In that case, you would not merely see a new car in your mind's eye. You must actually enter the dream. Feel yourself seated behind the steering wheel. Smell the newness of the interior. Feel yourself enjoying a comfortable ride. Feel the happiness that would be yours after accomplishing your dream.

That which you experience in imagination is an actual creative act. It is a fact in the fourth dimension of space and will make its appearance in this three-dimensional world just as surely as planting a seed will result in the growth of a particular plant. Once you have planted this seed in your imagination, do not uproot it by being anxious about how it will be accomplished. Each seed has its own appointed time. Some seeds take a few days; others a little longer. Feel confident that what you have planted will appear in your world. Your imagination will draw all that it needs to make your dream an actual reality. It if takes others to play a part in order to accomplish your end, your imagination will draw that person into your drama to play his or her part in the sequence of events. Your only responsibility is to remain faithful to your imaginal act until you experience it in your outer world. You can repeat your imaginal act each night before falling asleep. In fact, you may wish to enact this drama over and over again until it feels normal and natural to you as you drop off to sleep. Your imagination will work out the means to realize your dream while your conscious mind sleeps.

Bring your five senses into play as you perform your imaginal activity. Actually hear a friend's voice congratulating you or feel yourself hugging that person. If you wanted a new piano, run your hand over the smooth wood, touch the keys, and listen to the sound. If you wanted to receive a dozen roses, actually smell the fragrance and touch their velvety petals.

Finally, you must be persistent in attaining your desire. Continue to imagine what you want until you have actually obtained it. You do nothing else to obtain your desire. If it is necessary to take some action, you will be led to do so in a normal, natural manner. You do not have to do anything to "help" bring it about. Remember that it is God, Himself, who is doing the work and He knows exactly how to accomplish it. If you think of your desire during the day, give thanks that it is already an accomplished fact – because it is!

Dream better than the best you know.

One Cause

Nothing is impossible! There are two ways to interpret this statement – both of which are correct. The obvious meaning is that it is possible to achieve anything you want. It can also be interpreted to mean that it is impossible for nothing to exist. Everything we are aware of or perceive in some way is something. It is inconceivable that something can come from nothing or that something can become nothing. It is a fact that nature abhors a vacuum and always rushes in to fill it with something. Some force or power created all that is. According to the Bible, creation is finished. Not only is creation finished, but God said it was good.

Have you ever considered what God could have used to create all there is? If creation is finished, how is it possible to pray to God to create something in your life that did not exist yesterday or today? Is it difficult to believe that God said His creation was good? If all of creation is good, why do people experience problems and how can wars, crime, starvation and other undesirable conditions exist?

The answers to these questions are contained within the following pages. Your understanding of these answers will enable you to see that it is impossible for nothing to exist. You will also see that you can obtain anything you desire because nothing is impossible to the creative power that resides within you. You can be and you can have all that you desire to be and to have. There is no limit to what you can accomplish for yourself and others. It doesn't matter what your present circumstances are. The principle you have unconsciously used to bring about the undesirable conditions in your life can be consciously applied to make your every dream come true.

Creation is finished and it is good! God created the earth and all that is in it and God said it was good. Man has puzzled over these statements for centuries. If man really understood the meanings, he would not be confused nor would he feel anxious about his past, present or future. The understanding of these two statements would enable man to realize that he, alone, controls his actions and the circumstances of his life.

Let us take the first statement. God created the earth and all that is in it. God is infinite; therefore, God must have been before any form came into being. What substance could He have used to create all that exists?

There can be only one answer. God created everything that exists from the only substance available – Himself. God (thought/consciousness) spoke the Word and brought everything into being out of himself. Everything you perceive is made of the one substance – God. The one substance back of everything is energy and that energy is God or the "Word."

Although scientists and medical men can analyze the various chemicals of which the body is made, none can combine these chemicals to form a living person. Since God created all that is out of Himself, it follows that God is the creator and the creation. God is expressing life through each and every one of us. It could not be otherwise.

Let us take the second statement. God said that His creation was good. That statement has confused man who believes that if God is good, another power must have created that which is not good. Yet, man also acknowledges that God is infinite, omnipotent, omnipresent, and omniscient. These qualities of God must include all forms, all events, and all situations. If it were possible to remove all that is discordant or inharmonious from the world, it would not be possible to experience the reverse of that condition.

Perhaps this statement can be understood more easily if you will think of the principle of mathematics. In adding the sum of five and six, it is possible to obtain the incorrect answer of twelve. To eliminate that possibility, the number twelve would need to be removed from the whole of numbers. It would, therefore, be impossible to add six and six and reach the correct answer of twelve. You can see that by eliminating the possibility of a potential wrong answer, all numbers would eventually be eliminated and mathematics would not be possible. However, just as mathematics exists and can be used by anyone who has gained an understanding of how to use the principle to obtain correct answers, so the principle of creation can be understood to obtain desired results.

Because God has given all of us free will, you can choose the states you wish to occupy. God does not pre-determine your fate nor does God punish you for mistakes or misdeeds. Because a man may not understand the law of mathematics, he may be adversely affected when he makes a mistake in subtracting an amount in his check register. The law of mathematics is not punishing him. The law simply is and can be used correctly or incorrectly. God has allowed you complete freedom to choose that which you will encounter. When you come to the realization that you are God in form and expression, you will seek to experience greater good and nobler purposes for yourself and others.

"In the beginning was the Word and the Word was with God and the Word was God." The Word is thought or imagination. God imagined the world into being and became that which He conceived. This is the principle on which all creation rests. Since God became man to give man life, man must contain that same creative principle within himself. "The Kingdom of Heaven is within you." We have created our personal world through thought. If you are experiencing lack, limitation, illness, disharmony or any other unwanted condition, you have either consciously or unconsciously brought these conditions into your experience. The majority of people do not realize that thought, belief, and imagination has created their individual worlds. There is no other cause for the conditions of your life. You may choose to disbelieve this, but whether you believe it or not, all that you behold in the outer world was conceived within your own consciousness prior to your experience of it.

That which you think about with feeling, that which you believe to be true and that which you imagine yourself to be or to have is the cause of everything in your personal world. You may believe that there is some other cause; you may blame others for your problems; you may believe that the events were wrought by fate or chance, but if you are objective and observe your own beliefs and thought patterns, you will see that your world accurately reflects all that you believe to be true of yourself and others. There is no one and nothing to change but the ideas from which you think. We think from ideas that we consent to as true and we imagine situations that match our beliefs. Consciousness is the only reality. It is the creative principle that brings into your experience the exact duplicate or reflection of that which you imagine to be true. The world in which we live mirrors all that we believe and imagine to be true, be it good, bad, or indifferent.

The sooner that man rids himself of the belief in a second cause, the sooner will he realize that nothing happens to him except that which originates in his own consciousness. I do not deny that man believes that if he contracts a certain germ or virus that he will manifest a particular illness or disease. If he contemplates the cause, he may conclude that it is because he came in contact with someone else who had the bug. He doesn't realize that in some way, his own feelings about health or illness attracted the illness he is experiencing. If viruses or germs were truly the cause of disease, everyone who came in contact with a particular virus would be affected. The outer world merely reflects that which a man is in his own consciousness.

It doesn't matter what you have been taught; you can change your beliefs and so change the circumstances of your life. The Bible states that when you pray, believe that you have received and you shall have it. Most of us have read that statement or heard it at some time. Few people have actually prayed in that manner. Have you ever been ill and prayed for health? If you needed money, did you believe when you prayed that you already had the sum you asked for? Most people pray to God to change something in their lives or to give them something they do not have. If their prayers were not answered, they think that God had a reason for withholding that particular thing. They think that perhaps God didn't grant their request because He didn't want them to attain their desire for some reason known only to God. Man sometimes thinks that God doesn't answer prayers because man is undeserving of that which he seeks. Man must learn to believe in that which he does not, at the moment, see in order to grant himself that which he desires to have. Man's payers are always answered, for he always receives that which he believes. The law that governs prayer is impersonal. Belief is the condition necessary to realize the desire. No amount of pleas or ritual will bring about the fulfillment of your desires other than the belief that you are or have that which you want.

"Faith is the substance of things hoped for, the evidence of things not seen." The full meaning of that statement must be understood. If the meaning were understood, man would have no problem in accomplishing his aims. Most men believe that nothing is impossible to God – that God could do anything if he chose to do it. So man believes he has faith in God and prays to God for that which he wants. If his prayer is not granted, he thinks that he either did not pray long enough or hard enough or that God chose to withhold his request.

However, faith is the actual substance of that which is hoped for. It is the evidence of the thing you want which you do not see in the outer world. That which you want to do or be has already been created. Therefore, it actually does exist. It is possible to bring into your world anything in creation by your belief that you already have it. Faith that what you want is already a fact is the means by which you activate the invisible state. That state then is later reflected in your outer world. Creation is finished. God can create nothing that is not already existent. Faith or belief that you already are or have that which you desire is the only means by which to experience your desires. No limitation is imposed on that which you can have except your failure to assume possession of the quality or thing desired

How the Law Works

The law of identical harvest or cause and effect is impersonal and can be used to bring into your experience anything you can conceive. Since creation is finished, every possible state already exists. Your fusion with a particular state (imagining with feeling what you would experience were you in that state) causes that state to be projected on your screen of space. This law cannot be changed or broken and always reproduces in your outer world the exact duplicate of any belief you consent to as true. If you would change your world, you must change your beliefs. Since consciousness is the only cause, you cannot blame others for the conditions which presently exist nor can fate or chance be the cause of that which you are now experiencing. Nothing can alter the course of events in your life except a change in your own consciousness. Whatever is appearing in your world now, although it appears real and an unalterable fact, is a reflection of previous activity in your own consciousness. Therefore, a change in consciousness will reflect that change in the future just as surely as past beliefs reflect the present.

Man is pure formless consciousness and that which he conceives himself to be is an illusion or reflection of the particular ideas he holds true. These illusions exist only so long as man focuses his attention upon them and gives them life.

The conscious mind forms beliefs and opinions from the evidence of the senses or the perceived outer world. The creative power within each of us accepts as true that which the conscious mind impresses upon it. Your creative power takes those ideas, which are thought of with feeling, and projects them in your outer world. It is important to remember that not all thoughts are creative. Only those which are believed to be true or which are joined with feeling create the circumstances and events that you will encounter.

Therefore, emotions such as anger, fear, love or joy are creative. You must guard the emotions which you allow to enter your consciousness just as you would discriminate in allowing a stranger into your home. You cannot allow negative emotions to fill your mind without suffering the consequences of experiencing the state with which those emotions are joined. Fear of loss brings loss into your world. You could take every outward precaution to guard against loss, but if you fear loss, you will most certainly experience it in your affairs. Feelings of love and joy create happy events and loving relationships. Feeling abundant brings riches into your life. A person who is unloving or suspicious and feels that others take advantage of him, draws to himself that which he believes. No matter what he does externally, his relationships with others will reflect that which he accepts as true. He may want a loving relationship but he can draw to himself only that which he is conscious of being.

Like literally does attract like. As within, so without. Consciousness is reality and that which is perceived by our senses and appears so real is but the shadow of that which we believe ourselves and the world to be.

Conscious Use of the Law

At this time, I'm going to talk about who I am and what I am doing. If that sounds ego centered, it is. There have been 66 books written about who I am. I'm going to quote some statements from a few of those books. You have heard many of these quotes but didn't realize that they were talking about the being that I am. The first quote is taken from the

Book of Exodus. Here, Moses is talking to God and he said, "When I go back to the people, who shall I say has sent me?" The voice answers, "Tell them I am has sent me unto you. That is my name forever and the name I shall be known by throughout all generations." The Ten Commandments state, "Thou shalt not use the name of the Lord thy God in vain." "Shalt not" is a command. "Shalt not" means you must not. It means that under no circumstances must you do it. That name is I AM.

Now, first of all, we have all forgotten His name. We say, "I am" hundreds of times a day and we don't know we are using the name of God. Secondly, we try to break the Commandment all day long. We pay no attention to what we say following "I AM." When we say, "I AM" and follow it with something we would not like in our world, we are using the Name of the Lord – but not in vain. The Bible states we cannot use the Name in vain. Nothing we say preceded by "I AM" is in vain. That's his Name. It is God Himself and because it is God, it is creative. God gave us Himself. He is "I AM" and that is who I am. I can never forget that I am. I may forget who I am or where I am but I can never forget that I exist.

Whenever I say "I AM", I AM [is] creating something. Prayer is believing that we have already received that which we ask. When I say, "I am," I am attaching my awareness of being to something. Now, you can lie and not believe what you are saying, but you cannot believe something about "I am" and not create it. We are creating morning, noon, and night by our "I am" statements. If you say, "I don't feel well" and you believe it, you are perpetuating illness in your life. You must change those statements to "I feel wonderful." We were taught, "Let the weak man say, 'I am strong.'" But, you can't say it like a parrot. We have to pray (say I am), believing that it is true, and then we will receive.

First, we must be like the Watchman at the Gate. We must watch every thought that contains I Am. If you are observant, you will see that you have created every circumstance and experience of your life.

Another important word to watch is "if." The conscious mind is very subtle in expressing doubt (Satan or the Devil). We may be able to keep our minds focused on what we want by using positive "I" statements. If we are not careful, we may let a little "If" sneak in without recognizing its implication. We could say, "I feel wonderful" but then follow it with "If the pain continues, however, I will see a doctor on Tuesday." "If's" are always followed by something negative and that is simply doubt creeping in to steal the good seed we have sown. Remove the word "if" from your vocabulary, as it is not productive of that which you would like to reap. "If" puts everything in the past or future tense, and I always experience what I believe I am. I am is not future tense. Getting well is not being well. I must believe that I am already what I want to be.

Remember, "Every word that goeth forth from my mouth shall not return unto me void." Do you believe it? "In the beginning was the Word, and the Word was with God, and the Word was God." What's his Name? I Am. So, begin to monitor every word (I AM) that you say. Do you see a pattern? Don't the circumstances of your life reflect what you have been saying? You have been misusing the creative power that is God (I AM). Now that you are aware of what you have been doing, watch every word and make it conform to what you wish to bring into your life. Eventually, you will have faith that what you are stating, though there is no outward evidence to support it, is a fact in consciousness and will shortly project itself so that you may experience it in the outer. Knowing that God actually became you because He is I AM, you must realize that you are using your power to create every time you use that Name.

Choice – Free Will

Creation is finished and you have free will to choose the state you will occupy. Therefore, it is important to determine the ideas from which you think. Any concept that is accepted as true will externalize itself in your outer world. Choice of what you will focus your attention upon is the only free will that you can exercise. Once a thought is accepted and charged with feeling, the creative power within proceeds to externalize it. Whether your assumptions are conscious or unconscious, they direct all action to their fulfillment. It is a delusion that, other than assuming the feeling of the wish fulfilled, you can do anything to aid its realization. Your own wonderful human imagination determines the means it will use to bring your assumptions to fruition.

Each of us is subject to a sea of ideas. We listen to the radio, watch the news on television, or hear some gossip. If what we observe calls forth an emotion, we have reacted and, thereby, planted a seed which will sprout at some future time. Thoughts do not recede into the past. Rather, they advance into the future to confront us so that we may see that which we have planted, either wisely or unwisely.

It is a worthwhile exercise to awake in the morning and imagine yourself at the end of your day, having accomplished all that you wanted and feeling happy and contented. If there is a situation that you will encounter later in the day that is of concern to you, spend a few moments imagining the outcome you wish to experience. These imaginal activities will now advance into your future to reveal the harvest you so wisely planted.

Desire

Desire is a gift of God. Man is required to do nothing more than accept the gift by simply giving thanks for the unseen reality before he observes it in his outer world. Through desire, God beckons us to lift our awareness to higher and higher levels of consciousness. During our journey through this dream of life, it is necessary to experience all possible states so that we may return as God, the Father, but enhanced by having experienced both good and evil. The desire to do more, to be more, and to have more than you are presently expressing is the urge for expansion.

You may question whether a desire to kill or injure someone can be inspired by God. The answer is that no man actually desires to kill or harm another. He may wish to be free from that seeming other and, through his limited understanding, he feels that the only way he can achieve such freedom is by destroying the other. Man does not realize that the desire for freedom contains within itself the power and the means to fulfill itself. Because of his lack of faith, man distorts these gifts from God. He does not realize that God, the wisdom and power within him, has ways that he, as man, knows not of and those ways are past finding out.

Learn to be grateful for the desires you have been given. They already exist and are ready for embodiment in your world. You are not called upon to do anything to aid their realization except to free your mind of any doubt as to how they will come about and completely accept them as you would a gift from a loved one.

Be Observant

The importance of objectively observing your thoughts cannot be stressed enough. It is easy to slip into thought patterns that can hinder us in achieving our desires. It then becomes easy to blame others or attribute our frustrations to second causes.

Being a rather impatient person, I am usually anxious to get home after work and I particularly dislike waiting in lines. I began to notice that no matter what time I chose to pick up a few items at the market, I would encounter problems at the check stand such as price checks needing to be done, people writing checks who had trouble locating their identification, and various other kinds of delays. I found myself dreading these occasions, and I wanted to do something about this annoying situation. As I began to observe my thoughts, I found that, while standing in line, I would say to myself, "I always have to wait." Then I realized that those statements made over and over again had created that which I did not wish to experience. I consciously changed that statement to, "No matter when I stop at the market, I never have to wait." Of course that new statement has worked just as well as the old negative one.

As you begin to observe your thoughts, do not be discouraged if you find that your inner conversations do not match the way you would feel if you have achieved your goal. You must first become aware of what you are doing with your creative power before you can begin to change it. I ask you to go down to the "potter's house" and see what he is doing. If the vessel is spoiled, then rework it into the kind of vessel that will please you.

As you begin observing your thoughts, you cannot avoid the realization that you alone are the cause of all that comes into your world. You, alone, can change it.

Appearances

That which is confronting you in your world now is the result of your past thoughts, beliefs, feelings and imaginal activity. These appearances will continue in being as long as you give them life through your conscious awareness of them. You must disregard the evidence of your senses as it pertains to any undesirable condition in your life. You must imagine and feel that you have already attained that which you want to experience rather than that which you do not want to continue in being. This may appear difficult, yet you have probably exercised this principle unconsciously to produce negative results.

When I was in my early twenties, I found myself in a situation that was very unpleasant to me and I wanted to get out of it. After attending a lecture by Neville, I waited to speak to him afterwards. I briefly told him of my unhappy circumstances and was hoping he would offer some advice as to how to change them. He smiled at me and said, "Don't accept it." At that time in my life I did not fully grasp what Neville had been teaching. I thought he had misunderstood my question, and I tried to clarify my problem by stating that I had already made the choice to be in the situation I now found so unpleasant. Neville again smiled and said, "Don't accept it." I left his presence quite frustrated, thinking he had not understood my problem. I continued to read the two books I had by Neville. I gradually understood that regardless of the circumstances which surrounded me, I did not need to accept them as final. I began to imagine what I wanted rather than focus my thoughts on my negative surroundings. An event took place two weeks after I began my imaginal acts that was instrumental in bringing about my heart's desire five months later – that of a brand new home. Meanwhile, the situation that had been so depressing to me improved, and I spent the next five months planning what I would do in my new home.

Think about some past disappointment you may have had. Perhaps you were looking forward to attending a special event with someone. In your anticipation of it, did you think, "This is too good to be true, something will probably happened to spoil it." Something probably did happen to create conflict or to cause you to miss it entirely. Man finds it relatively simple to disregard the promise of something good by thinking of all the reasons why he cannot achieve it.

People around you may be quick to point out that you are being unrealistic when you mention a desire that appears difficult or impossible to reach. We should all be unrealistic in the face of the army of doubt if we would experience our wish fulfilled. We are called upon to disregard the "facts" which would deny the achievement of our heart's desire. Habit is the only thing that keeps our thoughts moving along the old familiar negative ruts. No one can change your thought patterns and, therefore, your life but you. It is worth all the effort it may take to center your attention and feel as if you already possess that which you want in place of things as they are. Consciousness is the only cause and the only reality. Every negative experience was produced by first giving attention and feeling to that condition. What consciousness has made, it can unmake. Your responsibility is to impress upon your mind the change you wish to express. Your imagination is the creative power that can and will accomplish the end without effort and in a natural way.

Appearances confirm our former habitual patterns of thought. That which you imagine yourself to be today will project itself in your world tomorrow. Persistence in assuming that you are the person you wish to be, despite your present circumstances, is the only condition imposed upon you to embody that ideal.

Inner Conversations

All of us are mentally speaking within ourselves every waking moment. Our inner conversations must match the wish fulfilled if we would realize our desire. If our desire is for a better job and we imagine ourselves being congratulated because we are gainfully employed in a wonderful position, we must also make our inner conversations conform to that end. We must be certain that we are not saying within ourselves something like, "That boss of mine doesn't believe in promoting people;" or "It would be difficult to find any job at my age, never mind a better one," or similar statements that would imply that we do not have that which we desire. We must persist in the feeling of our imaginal act by making our mental conversations conform to what we would say had we already realized our aim.

If, for instance, we wished to own a new car, we could imagine a new car parked in our garage or imagine ourselves driving it, or imagine our friends admiring it. We must then make our inner conversations reflect the type of conversations we would engage in were we really the owner of a new car. Our conversations could consist of discussing our new car with friends such as telling them of the wonderful fuel mileage we are receiving, or hearing our friends tell us how much they enjoy riding in our new car, etc.

Our inner conversations are just as creative as our deliberate imagining of the wish fulfilled. In fact, if they are of the opposite nature, they can negate what we have imagined. You must watch what you are saying internally to make sure that these conversations coincide with your wish fulfilled. If you become aware that these inner talks contradict what you would like to achieve, revise them so that they follow along the track that would indicate that you already have what you desire or are already the person you wish to be.

Revision

Your present world reflects the sum total of all that you believe to be true of yourself and others. That which you imagine yourself to be today goes forward and will confront you in the future. If you have forgotten your imaginal activities of the past, that which you see appearing in your world indicates the kind of seeds you have previously sown.

Assuming the feeling of your wish fulfilled is using your imagination creatively to bring into your world that which you desire to experience. You can use the art of revision to change the effects of prior thoughts and beliefs.

If, for instance, you had gone to an interview for a job you truly wanted but later learned that someone else was hired, you can revise that news to make it conform to what you wish you had heard. If you react by feeling depressed or assume any other negative attitude, you will then experience the same type of rejection in the future. Your reactions, whether positive or negative, are creative of future circumstances. In your imagination, you can hear words congratulating you on getting a wonderful new job. That imaginal act now goes forward and you will encounter this pleasant experience in the future.

As you review your day, it is important to revise each negative reaction so that you can remember it as what you wished had happened rather than storing that memory as it did occur. What you think of with feeling or emotion is an actual fact. That which you experience in the physical world is merely a shadow, reflecting the reality of your imaginal activity. Therefore, when you revise a conversation, an unhappy experience, or a quality about yourself, you are literally experiencing it in reality (your consciousness). The outer world is a delayed reflection of the inner and is confined to a dimension of space where events occur in a time sequence. Revision, then, literally changes the past. It replaces what occurred in the outer world with the revised version. The revised scene then gives off its effect by going forth to change future events.

Dwelling on past irritations or hurts perpetuates them and creates a vicious circle that serves to confirm these negative emotions. The circle can be broken by starting now to revise anything that you no longer wish to sustain in your world. By revising the past, you rid yourself of any effect it may have on your future. Revision is truly the key, which can be used to unlock the doors that have kept you trapped in a particular state. "Be ye transformed by the renewing of your mind."

States of Consciousness

All states exist and are a fixed part of creation. Anyone can enter a state consciously or fall into a state inadvertently. You may move into different states throughout your lifetime or you may occupy a single state. Desire is what usually motivates us to move from one state to a higher level. Since a state is total and complete in itself, when we enter a state we are compelled to behave in a manner dictated by that state. For instance, in the state of poverty, we would find ourselves constantly in need of funds. We would have difficulty making ends meet and have no way to enjoy luxuries. Should we be given a large sum of money, if we remain in the state of poverty (filling our mind with thoughts of lack and limitation,) we would soon find ourselves without funds and again experiencing the same difficulties. The reverse would be true if we occupied a state of wealth.

When we are in a state we see only the contents of that state and are compelled to act in accordance with all that the state entails. While in a particular state, you believe certain things are true and would find it difficult to understand another point of view. In the state of poverty, it is easy to focus your thoughts on the problems of providing food, shelter and clothing. When you succeed in moving out of this state, you no longer find it difficult to acquire these things. Most people attribute this change of fortune to a change in circumstances. However, unless you have moved from the state of poverty, no change in circumstance would be permanent. Rather, moving out of one state and into another in your imagination automatically creates a change in your outer world.

The Bible has personified every type of state and calls these states by names known to us as Moses, Noah, Job, Peter, Andrew, and Jesus. Throughout our journey, we enter these states and experience all that they offer. The last state we will enter is the state of Jesus Christ. In this state, we become aware that we are God, the Father, and that we have a son symbolized as David, who personifies the sum total of all humanity. The journey begins with Adam, who fell asleep and dreamed the dream of life, and then entered the myriad states to gain the experiences necessary before awakening. When you enter the state of Jesus you know yourself to be God, and your journey into this world of death is then complete.

The Play

As Shakespeare said, "All the world's a stage and all the men and women merely players. They have their exits and their entrances... and each man in his time plays many parts." This world, which seems so real, is as much a dream as the dreams we encounter while asleep. Our waking dream seems so real because it has continuity while our dreams at night appear to be random sequences, taking place in unfamiliar surroundings and situations.

God is the dreamer, dreaming the play into existence, and God plays all the parts. Everyone who appears in your world is God playing that part for you, the author. "No man comes unto me, save I call him." Each of us is writing his or her own script. If you are dissatisfied with the play, it is up to you to rewrite the script to make it conform to your idea of what the play should be. You cannot demand that the actors in your play change the character they are portraying. All changes must take place in the mind of the author.

If there is someone in your world who is the source of annoyance or irritation to you, that person has no choice but to play the part called for in your script. There is nothing you can do on the outside to bring about changes in another. You can use the art of revision to change a line of dialogue, to replace a certain character with another, and to write happy endings to the sub-plots of the play.

When you begin to view this waking dream objectively, you will be able to verify that you have been the author of both the pleasant and unhappy acts in your play. You can radically change the play by using your imagination creatively, by assuming your wish fulfilled. You can change the script on a daily basis by revising the scene that did not please you. The character who disturbed you today will not do so tomorrow if you write the dialogue you wish to hear and alter that role in your imagination.

When you awaken to know that you are God, the Father and author of this magnificent play, you will understand that: "each man in his time plays many parts."

Your Real Purpose

God became you so completely that he forgot that he was God. In becoming man, God reached the limit of contraction and opacity. God totally forgets that he is God in order to become and animate His creation, man. God then goes through all of the experiences of knowing good and evil and even death, in confidence, that man will eventually awake from this dream of life to once again know that he is God. There is only God in the universe, fragmenting himself as humanity, and God plays all the parts in this time-space dream.

Your own wonderful human imagination is God in action. I am is Christ in you (your savior). And Christ is the Power of God and the Wisdom of God.

God speaks to us through desire, urging us to reach higher and higher levels of awareness. Exercising his own wonderful human imagination to achieve these desires, man is actually experiencing God in action. Through faith in his imagination, man will eventually conclude that Christ (the Power and Wisdom of God) is within him as his imagination. At the end of this fabulous journey or dream of life, man will awaken to remember that he is God, the Father, enhanced by the experiences he put himself through; when he forgot that he was God. Man's sole purpose is to experience scripture (all of the states of consciousness personified as men in the Bible).

Man's goal is to reach the state called Jesus Christ. Then he will know that he really is the Father (Jesus) and that his son is Christ (all of humanity fused into one being). Man may have many goals in the meantime – to accumulate possessions, to become powerful, to become famous, or to express anything that he desires. Eventually the hunger to know God will come upon him, and he will then have the experiences that are necessary to bring to his remembrance that he truly is God, the Father.

Case Histories

This Story concerns a woman (who will be referred to as Mrs. A.B). She knew that "imagination creates reality" and had taught this principal to her three children, ages 12, 10, and 6. She had practiced this principal for years to obtain the things she desired. Although her husband had also heard this teaching, he had not put it into practice and actually was quite skeptical about results. One Sunday afternoon, this family went for a drive and came upon a new tract of homes for sale. As this was a lovely rural area, they stopped to look at the new models. They all loved the area, and the homes were large and beautiful with all sorts of modern amenities. On the way home, they talked about how wonderful it would be to own a new home in this tract. They already owned a home; however, they had borrowed money on it and had very little equity that could be derived from its sale. The husband said that although he would like to buy the home, it was not possible as they could not raise the money required for the down payment. Even if they sold their present home, the real estate agent's commission would equal the little equity they would realize.

Mrs. A.B. told her husband that the only way they could obtain the down payment would be to sell their home on their own, thereby keeping the commission for themselves. The husband was very pessimistic about this but told his wife to go ahead and place an ad in the paper although he knew "it wouldn't do any good." He was sure that there was no chance of selling the house in this way. The wife placed a small ad in the newspaper advertising their house for sale.

A few nights later when the husband had gone to bed early, she and her children drove to the tract of new homes. She felt that if she could walk through the new house and capture the feeling of actually living there, she would obtain her "dream home." It was dark when they got there, but they found one of the houses unlocked. She and the three children walked through the house. The children decided on which bedroom each would occupy if they actually lived there. The mother instructed the children to actually sleep in the new house in their imagination that night, and she intended to do the same. For the next few days, they imagined living in their new home and taking walks in the woods that were adjacent to the tract.

That same week, a man answered the ad in the paper. He did not seem very enthusiastic about buying the house but returned later that day with his wife. He told Mrs. A.B. that they had decided to buy the house for the price she was asking. When Ms. A.B. expressed concern as to how they would go about placing the home in escrow, he told her that he was a real estate agent and would go through the company he worked for. This family received the exact amount of money necessary for a down payment on their new home. The escrow was very short, and the family moved into their new home a month later.

Mrs. A.B. knew that if she imagined herself sleeping in her new home, she would eventually sleep there in the flesh. Her children also learned how to obtain their heart's desire through the use of imagination.

Mrs. C.D. had recently been divorced and needed to work to support her children as her husband refused to pay child support. Although her lawyer suggested taking him to court for non-payment, the woman did not wish to do this. As part of the divorce settlement, she was awarded a very old and not very reliable car. One Friday night as she was driving home from work, it was raining very hard and most intersections were flooded. She was about a mile from her home when she stopped at a Stop sign. A truck coming toward her from the opposite direction went through the intersection, spraying a great deal of water as he drove past. The engine of the woman's car died and she was unable to start it again. She removed her shoes before stepping out of her car as the water was more than ankle deep. She raised the hood and began to dry off the distributor cap with her handkerchief. She was crying at this point and her tears mingled with the rain. She finally got her car started and managed to get home to her children. She realized that it was necessary to have a dependable car if she was to work and support her children. She had no money for a down payment on a newer car and she did not earn enough to make car payments.

She went to work the following Monday and a co-worker asked her to go to lunch. The co-worker had just purchased a new Pontiac Tempest and insisted that Mrs. C.D. drive her new car back to the office. Although Mrs. C.D. protested that she did not wish to drive someone's new car, she did get behind the wheel and drove back to work. While she was driving the new car, she captured the feeling that this was her car and she felt the thrill of owning it. For the rest of the week, while she drove back and forth to work in her old car. Mrs. C.D. imagined that she was driving a brand new car of her own.

The next Friday, Mrs. C.D.'s ex-husband called and asked if she would like to have a new car. This was the first time since their divorce several months earlier that he had offered to do anything for her, including paying child support. The ex-husband was now working for a new car dealership and told her that, as a salesman, he was eligible to buy a certain make of car for no money down and with very low monthly payments. He said he was willing to make the monthly payments in lieu of child support and asked her to come to the dealership to pick out the color she wanted. It just so happened that the make of car eligible for this special deal was a Pontiac Tempest, the same make and model as the car she had driven that belonged to her co-worker.

Mrs. C.D. was able to obtain, through her use of imagination, what she could never have obtained through her own efforts at that time. Her ex-husband, who had offered her no monetary support for months, was the avenue chosen to provide her with the car she needed.

This is the story of Mrs. E.F., who had a desire to live near the ocean and used her imagination to fulfill her desire. She did not wish to sell her present home but wanted to lease it for a year before making the decision to move to the beach permanently. Mrs.

E.F. told two of her friends about her wish. One friend, who had used the principle of imagination, told Mrs. E.F. that she would imagine visiting her at the beach in her new home. One week later, Mrs. E.F. traveled to Hawaii for a scheduled vacation. While there, she received a call from a friend who lived n San Diego. This friend told Mrs. E.F. that a perfect little house had just come on the market as a year-around rental and she thought this house would be perfect for Mrs. E.F. Her friend also said that this was a very desirable rental and that Mr. E.F. would need to make a decision immediately as the rental would very likely not be available when she returned from Hawaii. Mrs. E.F. told her friend to tell the owners that she would take it, trusting her friend's recommendation. Upon Mrs. E.F.'s return from Hawaii, she told her grown daughter that she had decided to rent a house at the beach in San Diego. Her daughter called her later that day and said that the mother of a friend of hers wanted to lease a house. The woman came by the next day, said she loved the house, and would like to lease it for a year. Mrs. E.F. gave notice at work and was able to move within a month. Since she was a nurse, she had no trouble finding a wonderful new job at a nearby hospital. Mrs. E.F. has since bought a house near the ocean and has spent 17 happy years living at the beach.

Mrs. E.F. imagined that she was living at the beach, and her friend imagined that she was visiting her there. They did this for one week. It is interesting that while she was on vacation in Hawaii, events moved swiftly to bring about her desire. She did nothing to find a new home nor did she do anything to rent her present home. Imagination was able to draw the necessary people into her life so that her wish could be fulfilled.

"What should be done after we have imagined our wish fulfilled? Nothing. " You think you can do something, you want to do something, but actually you can do nothing to bring it about. God, our own wonderful human imagination, knows what things are necessary to bring about our desires. It is only necessary to go to the end, to live in the end. "My ways are past finding out." "My ways are higher than your ways." If we trust our imagination, it will "accomplish all that we ask of it." Imagination can do all things

– have faith in it, and nothing shall be impossible to you.

This story concerns a young man (referred to as E.P) who was a wonderful athlete and was good at many different sports. During this particular time in his life, he became interested in paddling outrigger canoes. He joined a team and was soon competing in local races. In his second year of pursuing this sport, he was on a team that competed in the 50-mile race from Molokai to Honolulu. The Hawaiian outrigger teams usually took first place and were considered "unbeatable." E.P.'s team came in 7th and that was considered quite remarkable considering the great number of teams that competed from all over the world along with the Hawaiian participants. After this race, E.P. began imagining that his team had won the race. He spent the next year forming a new team, practicing, and building his own outrigger canoe. He was convinced that if he imagined himself winning the race, his team would come in first.

He, next year, his team and at least a dozen others flew to Hawaii from Southern California to compete in the annual race. There were several teams with much more experience who were considered likely to place in the top ten, although the Hawaiians were still considered the favorites. At the end of the race, E.P.'s team finished first, ahead of the Hawaiians and all the other teams. E.P. now holds a paddle engraved with the words "World Champion" which was given to him upon his team taking first place.

After winning this coveted title, this young man went on to coach other teams. He also began manufacturing paddles for outrigger canoes. His paddles are known throughout the world and are used by outrigger teams who are among the top teams in the world.

E.P. now makes his home in Hawaii and enjoys coaching teams, manufacturing paddles, fishing and sailing his own boat. He also uses his boat as an escort craft for the annual outrigger races.

Mrs. J.K. was living in her twin sister's home after having been divorced. Mrs. J.K. had three children, a son and girl and boy twins. Her sister and her husband had three boys. Needless to say, this was a crowded household. Mrs. J.K. was very desirous of getting married and living in her own home. She had been dating a man but decided that she did not wish to continue the relationship and broke it off. Many of her friends attempted to "fix" Mrs. J.K. up with eligible men they knew, but she was not interested in going on blind dates. Several of her friends commented that if she wished to meet an eligible man, she would need to get out and go places. The twins believed in the creative power of imagination, and they had a friend who also knew of the power of imagining. The three women determined that they would imagine a ring on Mrs. J.K.'s finger, which would imply that she was married. They did this for several weeks. During this time, Mrs. J.K. also imagined herself living in her own home. However, when she attempted to do so, she found herself imagining a home exactly like her sister's.

One day, Mrs. J.K. received a call from a friend who asked her to come to her home and help her wallpaper her kitchen. Mrs. J.K. agreed to help her friend who lived a few blocks away in the same tract of homes. While she was there, a male neighbor came to visit her friend. The friend introduced Mrs. J.K. to her neighbor. He later called Mrs.

J.K. and they began to date. Five months later, Mrs. J.K. married this man. The interesting part of this story is that all of these people lived in the same large tract of homes. There were only four homes in the tract of 1200 that had the same floor plan. Yes, this woman's husband owned one of the homes that had the same floor plan as Mrs. J.K.'s twin sister. Even though Mrs. J.K. imagined herself living in her own home, she had only been able to imagine herself living in a house identical to her sister's.

This is a story about the friend, Mrs. L.M., who had introduced Mrs. J.K. to her new husband. During their friendship, Mrs. J.K. had tried to explain the principle of imagination to her friend who was very doubtful that "it" would work. One day, Mrs.

J.K. asked her friend to come to one of Neville's lectures. Mrs. L.M. agreed to attend but was not at all convinced that imagining she had what she wanted would result in obtaining it. But, she decided to imagine a very simple thing – the receipt of a handkerchief. She imagined that someone had given her one and then dropped the whole idea. Much to her surprise, she received a handkerchief in the mail from the mother of a friend who came to her house for lunch while she was in town for a visit. This woman sent Mrs. L.M. a handkerchief with a thank you note. Mrs. L.M. was not only surprised when she received the gift, she became very frightened as she thought there was something supernatural about it. Mrs. L.M. had attempted to disprove that imagination produces the thing desired. When she received the handkerchief she had imagined, she interpreted it to be some sort of Black Magic and didn't want to know any more about this teaching.

I could relate hundreds of incidents involving dozens of people in which imagination was used to bring about the desired results. I have chosen just a few stories to illustrate that imagination can be used to solve all manner of problems and bring into your experience your every heart's desire.

The Game *of* Life

The game of life, like every game, is played within the framework of certain rules, and any violation of those rules carries a penalty. You and I are playing this game from morning to night, and should therefore learn its rules in order to play it well.

Ecclesiastes gives us this rule: "Even in your thought do not curse the king, or in your bed chamber curse the rich, for a bird will carry your voice or some winged creature tell the matter." And Mark gives us another, as: "Whatever you desire, believe that you have received it and you will." If you must believe you have received your desire in order to attain it, then you must start your game by believing it is finished. You must feel yourself into and partaking of your goal. And you must persist in that feeling in order to achieve it.

Now, another rule is said in this manner: "Cast your bread upon the water and you will find it after many days." In other words, do not be concerned as to how it is going to happen -just do it. This statement hasn't a thing to do with doing good as the world defines the word. Jesus was a carpenter. The word means one who produces from seed -as a flower, a tree, the earth.

The prophecy of the Old Testament is the seed which a carpenter called Jesus brings to birth. He comes not to abolish the law and the prophets but to fulfill them. The word, "bread" in the statement: "Cast your bread upon the waters," means to devour; to consume. Water is a euphemism for semen, that living water which carries the sperm of man. The creative act is psychological, not physical; yet the intentions are the same. You must cast your bread upon the waters with passion! You must be consumed with the desire and literally on fire with love for its possession, for an intense imaginal act will always draw unto itself its own affinity.

Winston Churchill departed this world a very successful man; however, during his life he had many failures. Then one day he made this discovery, which changed his life. These are his words: "The mood decides the fortunes of people, rather than the fortunes decide the mood."

Let me put it this way: The game of life is won by those who compare their thoughts and feelings within to what appears on the outside. And the game is lost by those who do not recognize this law. Being consumed by anger, they see no change in their world. But if they would change their mood, their circumstances would change. Then they would recognize the law behind their world.

There are those who are depressed all day long and remain that way all of their life. I remember back in New York City, when I would see certain people walking in my direction I would want to cross the street, because I did not want to hear their depressing stories. They would spend hours telling about their wife or husband, their children or grandchildren, and each story geared to depression. Never changing their mood, their world never changed. Seeing no change, they would not recognize a law between the inner world they maintain and the outer world of response.

But if you apply this law you can predict your future. Feel a new mood rise within you. Sustain it and soon you will meet people who embody this new state. Even inanimate objects are under the sway of these affinities. In a certain mood I have gone to my library and removed a book I have not touched in years. And when I casually open it, I find confirmation of my mood. A table, though remaining the same, will be seen differently based upon your momentary mood, for everything reflects it. It is your mood which decides your fortune, not your fortune that decides your mood. People feeling poor attract poverty, not knowing that if they felt rich they would attract wealth.

In the Book of Proverbs, it is said: "The spirit of man is the lamp of the Lord." Now, the lamp of the Lord is the light of the world. We contain that light; and nature -the genie -is our slave, fashioning the world as our mood dictates. By nature I mean all of humanity -the animal, plant, and mineral world. In fact, everything that appears on the outside is a slave of this lamp. Fashioned from within, this slave will fashion your world to reflect your thoughts; and no power can stop their fulfillment. Become aware of what you are thinking, and you will recognize a law between your mood and your surrounding circumstances. Then you will predict with certainty, because you know certain events -being in harmony with your mood -must appear. Everything -whether a living being or an inanimate object such as a book -must appear to bear witness to your mood.

Now, in order to play the game of life, you must know what you want to replace what you have. When you know what it is, you must assume the feeling that you have it. Although your reason and senses will deny its existence, persistence will cause your assumption to harden into fact and objectify itself upon your screen of space. Play the game this way. You may think it doesn't work, but that's because you have not tried it. You may believe the idea is stupid, but I tell you: the mood decides your fortune. Believe me, for I have proved this principle over and over again in my life.

It was Winston Churchill who galvanized the Western world by putting his words into practice. In spite of the horrors and bombing in London, Mr. Churchill sustained the mood of victory, and even in the darkest days he would not waver. Knowing the mood would externalize itself around the world, he sustained the mood while his opponents, not knowing the law, put their trust in armies and machinery of war.

Mr. Churchill's wonderful statement, recorded in the "New York Times," has proved itself to me. By simply catching the mood I have changed the circumstances of my life. Now I teach others how to do it. I invite you to ask yourself how you would feel if your desire was now fulfilled. Toy with the thought. Play with it a while and the mood will come upon you. Keep that mood by playing with the senses it evokes, and watch your world change to match your new mood.

Let me tell you of a lady I know who, in her middle sixties, had nothing when she put this principle into practice. Every morning as she soaked in the tub prior to going to her $75 a week job, she would say to herself: "Something wonderful is happening to me now." She kept playing upon the mood, toying with the feeling that something wonderful was happening. That very week she received her first breakthrough.

For thirty-odd years this lady had attended the opera, concerts, and Broadway shows, with an intimate friend. Every night they dined in some fabulous restaurant, but he had told her many times he would never give her any money. But he suddenly had a change of heart and signed over a one hundred thousand dollar trust fund to her, to be spent immediately as she so desired.

A short time later, she began to apply the law to a greater degree and he again set up another one hundred thousand dollar fund for her. Now, this lady -whose rent is $165 per month -can't spend the income she receives from a two hundred thousand dollar fund, plus her social security; but she isn't satisfied and wants more! The old gentleman has a little hardening of the brain now and they have parted company. And, because he refuses to see her, she curses him, though we are warned: "Even in your thoughts do not curse the king, or in your bed chamber do not curse the rich, for a bird of the air will carry your voice, or some winged creature tell the matter." This lady calls me every week to tell me she is overcoming the cursing. I hope so, because other things can come into her world if she continues to do so. The law has its positive as well as its negative side. I am not here to judge how you use the law, but leave you to practice it as you will. If you are in the habit of thinking negatively, you are not going to sustain the thought that you are all you want to be. You may hold it for a few seconds, and if it does not prove itself instantly you may deny it. But in order to play the game of life you must know the rules and apply them. And remember: as in every game, there are rules whose violation causes failure. You cannot deceive yourself, for God is not mocked; as you sow, so shall you reap.

In the world you may get away with a violation that the referee did not see; but you cannot get away from the observer in you, for he and you are one. If you know what you did, then he knows, for your awareness and the father of your world are one. You cannot deceive yourself. You cannot mock yourself. God is going to record your every violation and mold your world in harmony with your feelings.

Let me now share a letter I received from a friend. In it he said: "Last Monday night a friend asked me for help, so that night I spent a half hour imagining I heard the words he would say if his desire were realized. Just before I awoke the next morning, the friend's wife appeared in my dream and thanked me for my help. "Then Tuesday evening, while enjoying some music in my living room, my friend appeared in reverie. Speaking with authority, power, and joy, he used the identical words I heard when I imagined him confirming the fulfillment of his desire, and I felt the thrill of completion."

It is my hope that confirmation will come in the immediate present, and my friend will hear the man tell him in person of the fulfillment of that imaginal act which was set on fire by his friend. Now, in another part of his letter, my friend said: "In a dream I entered a hotel lobby, registered at the desk, and asked to be called at 7:00 o'clock the next morning. As I watched, the man marked a bold seven over my name on the card; then I awoke." This is a marvelous vision, as seven is the numerical value for spiritual perfection. It also has much to do with gestation and incubation. In the insect and animal world, I am told, that 280 days is a multiple of seven. We know that a hen's egg, if properly incubated, takes 21 days -again a multiple of seven. Here we find birth has multiples of seven, but in his case it is incubation of spiritual perfection.

Another lady wrote, saying: "I saw myself lying in bed, ghastly pale as though dead. Suddenly a giant of a man rose out of my body."

Let me tell you the story of a wonderful artist, who was also a mystic. His name was George Russell, but you know him best as A.E. He said: "I will tell this vision, but where it happened I will not say. It was a vast hall with the columns made of living opal as though the colors of dawn and evening had blended into something alive. Between the columns were thrones upon which fire-crested kings were seated. One wore a crest of the dragon, another, plumes of fire. In the center a dark body was stretched out on the floor as though in a deep trance. At the far end of the hall, on a throne higher than the others, sat a being with the sun's glory shining behind him.

As I watched, two crested kings rose, and stretching their hands over the body on the floor, sparks of light came out of them. Suddenly a figure as tall, as majestic as these fire-crested kings rose out of that dark body. Looking around, he recognized his kin and raised his hand in salutation. Then they leaped from their thrones, raised their hands in the same wonderful greeting and -like brothers -walked toward the end and disappeared into the sun."

Each vision is a foreshadowing of what will take place. A.E. perceived him as coming from another, while this lady saw him as coming from her own being. They are both adumbrations of a wonderful event which will take place in everyone; for that crested king, who is the Son of God, is housed in all.

It does not matter whether the body be that of a woman or a man, or what the pigment of the skin may be; within each one of us is the Son of God, who -radiating his glory and bearing the express image of his person -is the great lamp of the Lord. And one day this majestic being will rise out of your garment of death, and you will enter the land of life.

But while we are here, let us learn the rules of the game of life and play it. Life itself is caused by the assemblage of mental states, which occurring creates that which the assemblage implies. My friend mentally heard the words he would hear if his desire for his friend were fulfilled. Its assemblage, occurring within him, created the event to be played out in the game of life.

After you have assembled your mental state and allowed it to occur within you, you do not have to repeat the act. You cast your bread upon the water the moment you felt relief. Although you do not have a physical expression in a sexual manner, relief is possible; and of all the pleasures of the world, relief is the most keenly felt. When someone you dearly love is late, you anxiously await that key in the door. And when you hear their voice, your relief is keenly felt. That is the same kind of relief you will have when you have imagined correctly.

If you find it necessary to recreate the act every day, you are not casting your bread upon the water. You may imagine over and over again, but you are only going to impregnate once; and if you reach the point of relief, your bread has been cast upon the water to return, perhaps in the matter of an hour. I have had the phone ring -minutes after I have imagined it -to hear confirmation that it has happened. Sometimes it has taken days, weeks, or months; but I do not repeat the action once I have done it and felt the feeling of relief, for I know there is nothing more I need to do.

Learn to consciously play this game of life, for you are unconsciously playing it every day. I am sure the millions who are on relief feel the government owes them a living; but there is no government, only we who pay taxes. The government has no money and can only give what it takes from our pockets. Those on relief are complaining, claiming they are not getting enough out of our pockets, and that mood persists throughout their day.

Their mood never varies, so they see no change and recognize no law between the mood they are sustaining and the outer world they dislike. If they were told that their mood was causing the phenomena of their life, they would deny it. No one wants to feel that he is solely responsible for the conditions of his life, yet there is no other cause. God is the only cause and he is man's own wonderful human imagination.

When I speak of imagination I am referring to God in you, of which there are two sides: imagining and contacting. Contacts are what imagining is all about. When you imagine, you contact a feeling, and the feeling you imagine, you create. You are the same God who created the world and all within it, but while you are clothed in a garment of flesh and blood your power is keyed low.

I do hope you understand the rules to the game of life; and -because there is a positive as well as a negative rule -I urge you not to curse anyone. Ecclesiastes used the words "king" and "rich" because they are the ones most often envied. A person need not be a millionaire, however, to be envied. He could simply be a little bit better off than another. Someone could live in a better neighborhood, pay more rent, maybe even go to a better restaurant, or buy better clothes, to be envied. So we are warned not to curse the king or the rich in our thoughts, for they cannot be concealed, as all thoughts are completely one; and by a law divine they mingle in one another's being.

Awareness seems to be scattered, as everyone on the outside is aware. But no one needs ask another to aid in the change of his world if he changes it on the inside. If another is necessary to bring about the change, he will -with or without his consent. You do not have to single out the individual to play the part in bringing about the change you have imagined. He will play his part if necessary because we all intermingle. All you have to do is stand at the end, from within.

I remember visiting my family in Barbados, when I was told I could not leave the island for seven months; but I wanted to leave on the next boat out. To me, being on that boat was my end; so -while sitting on a chair in my parent's home -I entered the boat in my imagination and viewed the island as I was departing. I did not know how I would get on it, but a week later when the boat left the island I was there. This I know from experience.

In your desire to go anywhere you must first go there in your imagination, and even those who may deny your request will aid you when the time is right. I got out of the army that way. Knowing I wanted to be honorably discharged and in my apartment in New York City, I slept as though it had already happened and I was already there. Then my captain -who had previously disallowed my discharge -had a change of heart and aided in my release. Anyone can do it. This game is easy to play and can be lots of fun in the doing. Think of an object you would like to hold. Think of a place you would desire to be. Then find an object in that room and feel it until it takes on sensory vividness.

Don't make it a lamp, but that lamp; not a table, but that table. Sit in that chair until you feel the chair around you. View the room from that chair and you are there, for you are all imagination and must be wherever you are in your imagination. Now, cast your bread upon the water by feeling the relief of being there, and let your genie -who is your slave - build a bridge of incident over which you will cross to sit in that chair, hold that lamp, and touch that table.

In Genesis, the story is told of Isaac -who was unable to see, but capable of feeling -calling to his son, Jacob, saying: "Come close my son that I may feel you. Your voice sounds like my son Jacob, but you feel like Esau." At that moment Jacob -the imaginary, purely subjective state - possessed the qualities of Esau, the objective world. So Isaac gave the imaginary state the right to be born.

As Isaac, you can sit quietly and with your imaginary hands you can feel the difference between a tennis ball, a baseball, a football, and a golf ball. If they are nothing (because they are subjective and not objectively real to you at the moment) then you could not discriminate between them. But, if you can feel the difference between these so-called unrealities, then they must be real, although not yet made objective to your senses. The moment you give them reality in your mind's eye, they will become real in your world.

Try it just for fun. Take an object and thank the being within you for the gift. Then thank the one on the outside, for within and without are vicarious, as is life; for by observing an odor, a look, or a feeling within, you will discover you are life itself.

Yes, life is a game. Paul calls it a race, saying: "I have finished the race, I have fought the good fight and I have kept the faith." I call it a game. Both are competitive; but the opposition is with self and not with another, for there is no other. Do not try to get even with another. Grant him the right to use the same law to achieve his goal, even though it may be similar to yours. The knowledge you share will never rob you. Simply determine your goal. Feel you have achieved it and cast your bread upon the water. Then drop it and let the game of life be fulfilled in your world.

Now let us go into the silence.

The Hidden Cause

The dream of life unfolds on this level, as well as on a higher one. On this level we see things happen and are given reasons for wars and revolutions, as well as the geological causes for the convulsions of nature. But we do not know and cannot perceive their hidden cause, for it lies in the imagination of man. All things spring, not from the ostensible causes to which they are attributed, but from that which is hidden -man's own wonderful human imagination!

In the April issue of the Atlantic Monthly, there is an article by General David M. Shoop, retired commandant of the Marine Corps. In this article, he claims that there is an ambitious elite of high-ranking officers who are turning this country into a militaristic and aggressive nation. They are promoting war in the belief that through it they will receive the promotions and glory they desire and cannot achieve while serving in a peacetime army. They dream of a war they can command in glory. Where? In their own wonderful human imagination, the hidden cause of all life! Imagination can be used infernally -as these men are doing -or towards the kingdom of heaven. This is done by thinking of a friend and hearing him tell you his good news. You can watch his facial expression change as he speaks to you. You can see him stand erect, wearing clothes he is proud of, as you feel the thrill of his change. And if you will believe that what you are now seeing is real, you can relax in the knowledge that one day your friend will conform to what have you done in your imagination!

Do you know that you can take that same individual and hear him tell you sad news? You can see him dirty and ashamed, and he will conform to that image which you have created in your imagination? Your creative power, which is Christ, can be used infernally or in a heavenly way. Its use is entirely up to you. General Shoop claimed that our involvement in Vietnam was a direct result of the ambition of an elite group of high-ranking officers who prefer war to peace, in order to receive glory and prestige in their chosen field! You and I are now burdened with the enormous task of continuing their effort, which began in the imagination of a small group of men.

The prophets and poets, inspired by the same voice, have told us this throughout the centuries. Yeats said: "I will never be certain that it was not some woman treading in the winepress who started that subtle change in men's mind. Or the passion, from which so many countries have been put to the sword, did not begin in the mind of some poor shepherd boy, lighting up his eyes for a moment before he ran upon his way." Who knows who is treading in the winepress this night? Who knows what a person in solitary confinement is imagining? Is he using this only power in the universe infernally or blissfully? I hope you use your imagination in the state of bliss, for the outside world is alive because of this hidden power within you. I know that a man, imagining intensely can influence millions. He can act through many men and speak with many voices. This little group of men, imagining their promotions, are influencing millions and moving through unnumbered men toward their goal. Those who cover their costumes with medals, like the Stalins and the Hitlers of the world, are displaying their complete misunderstanding of God's power of imagination.

I ask you to believe me, for I am speaking from a level of one who has awakened from the dream of life. I have experienced scripture and know it is a true story from beginning to end. The gospel tells us of a pattern which repeats itself in everyone, for every child born of woman has within him an ancestral self, a heavenly being who supports him. This is the one who said: "I will never leave you or forsake you." A child is alive because a son of God -who is the emanation of that ancestral self -is in it. We are told that bounds have been set to the peoples of the earth according to the number of the sons of God. You were given the gift of awareness because of the immortal son of the ancestral you who will never forsake you, not in eternity. See how precious you are in the eyes of he who is the power of powers?

Now, do not misuse this power, but use it only in love. Every person you meet, regardless of his pigment of skin, the nation behind him, or the so-called sect he is associated with, is alive because your ancestral being who has no beginning and no end is behind his mask, as he is behind yours. That one is taking him through the necessary experiences to make him one with himself, as the ancestral you is taking you through the necessary experiences to make you one with himself. Eventually you and he will return to that one being who sent you out in the first place. That is your destiny.

Now, in the gospels we are told that the Risen Christ turned to his apostles and said: "There are those standing here who will not taste of death until they see the kingdom of God." Scholars claim this prophecy failed because they do not know what or where the kingdom of God is. It is not a realm, but a body. And it is not out there, but within. If, as Luke tells us, the kingdom of heaven is within you, who would know you entered it but yourself? And if you told your friends and it was not what they expected, would they believe you? No! They would continue to claim the promise was not fulfilled, yet I say the promises of God will not be broken. There are some standing here who will not taste of death before they enter the kingdom of God.

The kingdom, being within, is entered when the curtain is split. Only then can you see the blood of your ancestral being who died to become as you are. Recognition causes you to fuse with it, and rising like a fiery serpent, you enter that holy sepulcher where the drama began. Matthew knew that the violent took the holy sepulcher by force. The word translated "violent" here means "life; to press oneself into; to find a place within".

Life is in the blood. Contemplating the blood of God Himself, you fuse with it and become life itself. The Father, having life in himself, has granted you his emanation to be life itself. Becoming one with your ancestral being, you are no longer the emanated, but the Godhead through which the emanation occurred. So the statement is true: there are some standing here who will not taste of death before they enter the kingdom of God. But the only ones who will know it are those who experience it. This goes on forever and ever. If you are looking for the kingdom of God on the outside you will look in vain, for the kingdom is within and cannot be entered from without. In his 16th chapter, Matthew claims they will see the Son of man entering his kingdom, but in the 9th chapter of Mark and Luke, it is called the kingdom of God.

Now, after making the statement that some standing here will not taste death before they enter the kingdom of God, Peter, James, and John are taken into a high mountain where his countenance is completely altered before them. You may think this took place on the outside, but it takes place within. The evangelists took this appearance of resurrection and recorded it as Jesus' external ministry; just as when I tell you what happened in me I speak externally, yet the three people who witnessed my transformation appeared within.

Recently a lady wrote telling of finding herself in a cage, observing three men etched in gold, and a woman holding an infant. This is a perfect adumbration. The three first appeared to Abraham in the Book of Genesis, and were confirmed in Peter's second letter, where he remembers when Peter, James, and John were formed to witness the majesty of the one who was born. There are always three. The cage in which this lady found herself is the holy sepulcher, her immortal skull - where the drama began, and where it comes to its fulfillment. She saw the sign of her approaching birth from above, in the form of a woman holding a child and the three witnesses to this event. She -the emanation of her ancestral being -will awaken in that cage to return to her ancestral being, enhanced by becoming one with her celestial self.

While in this world of Caesar, seemingly detached and lost, you are not, for your human imagination is a wonderful power. It is yours to use lovingly, or as unlovingly as those men did with their dreams of wars, in order to get a little medal and be promoted. So what if they do? Eventually they will all be buried, and two generations later no one will know they ever existed. Our cemeteries are filled with monuments to those who thought themselves so important, yet no one recalls who they were. So I say: what does it matter if you own the world and lose your life?

I urge you to seek the kingdom of God, for when you do, you come into a power unknown to mortal man. All of the atom bombs in the world cannot compare to the power you are destined to fall heir to. You will possess a power that can still the world. But you will never know this power without love. With this power, unrestrained, you would still a nation, face its inhabitants toward the ocean, and put the idea of entering it in their mind. Then when you release this power they would all march into the ocean. But you will never know a power greater than you know love. The power known to earthly man is nothing compared to the power of love. With that power you can stop the thought process of another, change it completely, and when you allow that energy to flow once more, he will move in a different direction, not even realizing that a change had taken place within him.

When the embodiment of reason asked the Risen Lord: "Do you not know that I have the power to crucify you and the power to set you free?" Imagination replied: "You have no power over me were it not given you from above." Just imagine knowing you have that kind of power! You came to play a part called Man, and when you have experienced it, you will play the part called Jesus Christ. His play takes place in heaven, which is within. And when you tell your story, those who hear your words on the outside will either believe or disbelieve you, and you will have no power to persuade them otherwise. Those who do not believe sit in darkness, breathing war as recorded in this month's Atlantic Monthly. Although the salaries of these men come from the pockets of civilians, they are believing our country into a militaristic and aggressive nation, in order to become more glorious in their own little minds.

But I tell you, your ancestral being called the son of God shed his blood for you that you may have life in yourself. I know, for when my body was torn in two from top to bottom, I saw that blood of God as my own wonderful ancestral self. I am an extension of that self, not another - for that would imply there was a greater creative power than I am. I have seen this body of love. I wore it when we embraced. I will return to it and wear it forever when I leave this body of death for the last time. Then we will not be two, for I -an extension of myself -will return to myself, adding to God's glory, His luminosity, and translucency, giving him a greater creative power by reason of the part I played, called Neville.

I urge you to use your imagination lovingly on behalf of everyone, and believe in the reality of your imaginal acts. If you have a friend who would like to be gainfully employed, listen carefully until you hear his voice tell you of his new position. Feel his hand clasp yours. See the smile on his lips. Use every sense you can possibly bring to bear into the imaginal scene. Persist until you feel the thrill of reality, then drop it and let that scene fulfill itself on the outside. We are told that the kingdom of heaven is like a mustard seed. Your imaginal act created for your friend in the kingdom of heaven is that seed. Don't pick it up to see if it is growing; just leave it alone, and it will grow and bloom as a solid fact in your world. Then you will have found this hidden cause within you called Christ.

Christ, the power and wisdom of God, is in you as your own wonderful eternal being. He will never leave you or forsake you as told us in the 13th chapter of Hebrews. If, perchance, one day you are swept into an unlovely state and go through hell, remember: there is that in you who will not leave you or forsake you; and if you know this principle you can detach yourself from the state and it will vanish, as you move into a more desirable one.

There is truly nothing new under the sun. That which was recently recorded in the Atlantic Monthly is the same as that which was recorded in Genesis as the first frightful act, when Cain slew his brother Abel. This same act is taking place over and over again, and if a man knows how to detach himself he need not be pulled into that state. While in the army I was told I could not get out, but I dared to assume I was out. I acted, in my imagination, as I would act were I free to come and go as I chose. I persisted in this assumption for nine days. Then the one who first denied my request granted my freedom, and that day I was honorably discharged.

People plan a depression for personal gain. There are those who sell short for a personal gain. All kinds of things are done in order to be known as a billionaire; yet in time they die, to leave their billions behind for those who can't even remember their names. Leaving this little section of time, he who was known as a billionaire here, moves into another section of time to once more seek his fortune. So the words are true: there are some standing here who will not taste of death.

May I tell you: no one can leave this earth until he awakens, because the earth does not terminate at the point where the senses cease to register it. When you shed your little garment, you will still be on this earth in a body like the one you left behind, only young, vital, and wonderful -but your environment will change. You may leave this world a billionaire to find yourself shining shoes, if that is to be your lot to fulfill. Your ancestral being knows what it will take to weave you into the likeness of himself, for you must be perfect as he is perfect. You will not be brought to the end until you can actually be superimposed upon his image and fit it perfectly. Then you are one!

No one ever leaves this age of death until he awakens. This earth stretches for a length of time long beyond the three score and ten. The world remains terrestrial, with all of its struggles. We continue to marry and die, to know sickness and health, sorrow and joy, just as we do here, as we go from one little section of time into another and then another until -in the eyes of our ancestral self -we are as He is. So you see that statement is true: "There are those standing here who will not taste of death." The apostles who are called will not taste of death. No power can sweep them away from this section of time, until they go up that spiral roadway into the sepulcher where their drama began.

No mortal eye can see the kingdom of heaven, and it cannot be entered from without, but must be taken violently. This I know from experience. When I went up, it was with such force I felt a tremendous pressure in my head where I was pressed in, just a little bit left of center. I tried my very best to go beyond it, but I could not. It was so crowded I pressed myself right into the kingdom as a living mural, having entered it with a force akin to violence. I have now fulfilled the 11th chapter of the Book of Matthew: "The kingdom of heaven is taken by violence and the violent take it by force." The old age of the law and the promise up until John the Baptist is behind us now. There is no need to do violence against your body in order to get into the kingdom. No diet or suppression of the normal urges of life will get you in. Only when you are one with your eternal self so that you can be superimposed upon him and fit perfectly will you find yourself split in two to be absorbed by the life of the being who kept you alive here as something on the outside and, like a sponge, you become one with it. Then, having life in yourself, you will return to your skull where the dream began, arriving with such force your head reverberates like thunder. But, knowing that there are people in this world who plot and plan violence, don't try to compensate; rather plot and plan things of love and affection. Do that and you cannot be drawn into another's circle.

I tell you: you are an immortal being. You were the Son of God long before the universe came into being. It was you who brought it into appearance for this great experiment. You are a ray of the being you really are, one with He who is radiating you. And He will not forsake you, but will continue to put you through the paces as He fashions you into his likeness. Then He receives unto himself all of the experiences through which you will have passed, and is enhanced and glorified by them. He is afflicted as you are afflicted. He suffers as you suffer, and when you return you and He are one, for the being radiating is one with the ray.

Take me seriously! Know what you want and then claim you have it. Tell a friend about it and feel his excitement for you. Persuade yourself that what you are imagining is true. Believe in its reality and it will come to pass as an objective fact on this level, I promise you. Then when the image is perfect, you will return to your ancestral self, and time will no longer be necessary between the imaginal act and the fact.

There are many levels: a level here, a dream level, and a level of spirit waking, where every thought is a fact and is known. From that level you return through various barriers to this, the lowest level, where everything is completely concentrated and limited in these little garments of flesh. Here we are slaves to our mortal bodies, serving them morning, noon and night as we feed, clothe, and shelter them. When you feed your body you must assimilate what it eats. Then you must eliminate its waste and care for it.

Every child born of woman is a slave to the body he wears. There is no slavery comparable to the slavery of the body. If I were a slave to one who had purchased me and I must feed and clothe him, though he has millions and I have nothing, he is as much a slave to his body as I am to mine, for he and he alone must assimilate and eliminate for himself. No matter how many slaves he may have, he cannot command them to perform the functions of his body for him. He must perform them all for himself. Everyone who comes into this world becomes a slave to the body he wears.

We are told in Philippians: "He emptied himself of all that was his and became obedient unto death, even death upon the cross." When God came here he found himself a slave and was born in the likeness of men, thereby entering slavery. And I can't conceive of any slavery comparable to the slavery of the body. Just imagine: you must wash it, shave it, bathe it, and do everything for it. And when it begins to wear out, you must get glasses for its eyes, false teeth, hearing aides and heart transplants -to name but a few. You must continue to patch it up while remaining its slave to the very end. Do you know of any greater form of slavery?

While in our teens and twenties we never think that our body might get old and wear out, yet one day we turn a little corner of time and it becomes so obvious. Although the body wears out and becomes weaker and weaker, you are still its slave. I cannot conceive of any greater slavery.

But try to live a noble life, for you are immortal and cannot die. He who radiates you will never in eternity forsake you. He could not, for you and He are one; and when you return from your journey, you will be with the one who radiated you, just as you were before the journey began.

Now let us go into the silence.

The Mystery *of* Life

The words of one in whom the great mystery of life unfolded, are enigmatic. And the evangelist who wrote the gospels, kept that great mystery as it was told. In the 17th chapter of the Book of John, he is speaking to God the Father, the depth of himself, saying: "Now I am no more in the world, but they are in the world and I am coming to thee. Holy Father, keep in thy name that which thou hast given to me that they may be one, even as we are one." (The only name that can bind us together and make us one is Father. When you and I discover that we really are the Father, we will understand the mystery of life.) Now he makes this statement: "I have guarded them and none is lost but the son of perdition that the scripture might be fulfilled."

Bear in mind, this is not secular history, but salvation history; so who is this son of perdition that is lost? Scholars claim it is one called Judas, but that is not true. If you want to get close to the answer, read the 18th Psalm, which is repeated in the 22nd chapter of 2 Samuel. This is a hymn David sings, praising the Lord for saving him from death and destruction. And the word "perdition" means "death and destruction."

Let me take these enigmatic words and show you what they really mean. The son of perdition is one who hears, but refuses to accept, the Christian revelation. The 2nd chapter of 2 Thessalonians tells us that: "The lawless one, the son of perdition, will be revealed and the Lord Jesus will slay him with the breath of his mouth and destroy him by his appearing and his coming."

I tell you salvation's story as I have experienced it. You may deny my words, or agree with them. Those who deny me are the anti-Christ, the son of perdition. They themselves will not be destroyed, for the mystery of Christ will unfold in them.

Rather, the state of consciousness in which they dwell, will be lost, to them "for none have I lost but the son of perdition." No individual will, or can be, destroyed, for he is a son of God. He can fall into the state known as the son of perdition, and while in it, completely deny this incredible story is true. But when it awakens in him and becomes true, then he has nowhere to go but to admit the experience.

If I tell you the incredible story and you think it is silly, I am not concerned, but confident it is going to happen in you; and when it does, what you thought before does not matter.

And so it is with others that come after you: When they are confronted with the experience, their thoughts and beliefs change. Everyone will be saved, and the only thing that is lost is the state of consciousness in which the individual lived when he heard salvation's story and could not accept it.

The son of perdition has nothing to do with any Judas, for he is the one who betrays the messianic secret. No one could ever betray you but yourself, for no one knows your secret but yourself! Judas is Judah, the Lion's whelp. He is the only son named in the genealogy of Jesus. "Jacob was the father of Judah and his brothers." Judah is the one who knows and tells the secret.

The son of perdition is not an individual man who can be destroyed, because every child born of woman is a son of God; and it takes all of his Sons to form God, as told us in the 32nd chapter of Deuteronomy: "He has put bounds to the peoples according to the number of the sons of God." And every child born here is an emanation of a son of God.

The word "Elohim," translated "God," is a plural word. We are told that "In the beginning God (Elohim) created the heavens and the earth, saying: `Let us make man in our image." Then the gods (Elohim) came down and buried themselves in humanity, and not one son can be lost, only the son of perdition, the state of consciousness which rejects and denies the Christian revelation.

You may question how a man can be consumed in the fire, turn to dust, and yet survive; but I tell you: all things are restored to life by the seed of contemplative thought, even the little discarded flower. That is restoration; but I am speaking of resurrection where the son is resurrected, not the body of flesh and blood he wears here. He who occupies a body that is always restored, is a son of God going through the world of death. And when his journey is over, he awakens from his great dream of death by the signs of life that follow.

Now, calling himself the son of man, Jesus speaks of himself in the future, saying: "When the son of man comes, will he find faith on earth?" Jesus is always coming, always awakening, in man. The great mystery called Christmas is the beginning of the signs of faith of which many will reject, as told us in the 2nd chapter of Luke. When Simeon took the little child in his arms he called it a sign for the fall and rising of many in Israel saying, "Thoughts out of many hearts will be revealed." This is true, for I have told the story and some have accepted it while others have disbelieved.

But even those who deny it now will one day pull themselves out of the state of perdition by finding Jesus rise in them as their very being. Then, by the breath of his mouth (the word of God), perdition will be slain by the sword of the Spirit, which is the Word of God, for the Word cannot return void. It must accomplish that for which it was sent. The gospel is the Word of God which actually became you that you may become the Word. Sending himself into the world as sons, God raises himself back to the awareness of being the Father.

Now he tells us, "When you see me you have seen the Father." How can this be? When you see me you know me to be yourself. You will never see the Father outside of yourself. If anyone should come saying, "Lord, there he is, or here he is," do not believe him for you will never find God outside of yourself. He will rise in you and you will know him only when his only begotten son, David, stands before you and calls you Father. Then and only then can you say, "I have found David, the son of Jesse (I AM), a man after my own heart who will do all my will."

In the state of consciousness called the son of perdition you cannot believe my incredible story. But the state will be destroyed by the breath of his mouth, as his Word unfolds in you. Although you denied it prior to the eruption of the Word in you, after you experience all that is said of Jesus Christ, you know you are he, and you cannot deny it. So the son of perdition is the only one that is slain, the only one that is lost. It's part of the play.

Everyone called by any name is saved, because it has already happened and will continue to happen; for I am in them and they are in me. Holy Father, keep them in thy name which thou has given me. That name is Father. I have kept them in the name thou gavest me by telling them that they are the Father, and they are moving towards the discovery of it. Although some did not believe me, I have guarded them and none of them is lost but the son of perdition, that the scripture (which is thy Word) might be fulfilled. I told them thy Word as I experienced it. I interpreted thy Word to them, and Father -they heard it. Some rejected it and some believed it. In spite of those who rejected it, may I say: they cannot die, for they are my brothers as we came down into this fragmented state together.

In this morning's Los Angeles Times Book Review section, several of Robert Grave's poems were printed. As I read them this one little verse stood out and my heart jumped within me. These are the words, if I recall them correctly:

"Hold fast with both hands To that Royal love which alone As we know certainly, Restores fragmentation into true unity."

What a revelation! The great poets are the ones who see so clearly. And those who have the capacity to use words, as Robert Graves has, say it so beautifully.

In the world the One is fragmented into the many. Regardless of the pigment of your skin, your race, your nation or belief, the world is the fragmented Rock that I saw back in 1934. During that time I was a dancer. The country was in the deep depression, and people could not afford to pay to be entertained by a dancer.

I lived in a basement apartment on 75th Street in New York City, not knowing where the next dollar was coming from. I did not despair, however, but sat in the silence and quietly closed my eyes. I was not thinking of anything in particular, just resting with my eyes shut, watching the golden clouds which always come, as all the dark convolutions of the brain grow luminous. As I contemplated this golden, liquid light, a quartz approximately 20" in diameter suddenly appeared, then fragmented itself into numberless parts. As I watched, they gathered themselves together into a human form seated in the lotus posture. Startled, I realized that I was looking at myself -but a self containing such majesty of face and beauty of features, that I could never have believed possible. There was nothing I could have added to that perfection to improve it.

I was looking at myself in deep meditation, not as a piece of clay, but a living statue. Then it began to glow and increased in luminosity until it reached the intensity of the sun and exploded; and I awoke to find myself still seated in my chair in my little basement apartment in New York City. Turning to scripture, I read the 32nd chapter of Deuteronomy: "Of the Rock that begot you, you are unmindful and of the God who gave you birth you are unaware."

Then in the 10th of 1 Corinthians, I read: "They drank from the spiritual Rock which followed them, and the Rock was Christ." Now I know that within all is Christ, the Rock that never fails.

Back in 1929, the market broke, and 17 million men were unemployed. At that time we only had a population of maybe 130 million, whereas today we number 204 million. Our bins were filled, but people could not pay the tax or get the money to distribute the food.

By 1934 I had already gone through five years of the depression, so I wasn't worrying about my next meal, or my next job for that matter. I was just resting, for by this time depression was a state of mind. So, as I daily did, I sat in my chair and turned my attention inward, into my brain, and contemplated within.

Then, as always, the clouds began to appear, grow luminous, and move in lovely, billowy, golden liquid light. Then came the rock. The perfect imagery of scripture. And the Rock was Christ. He formed himself into me, but me as a perfect being.

Everyone is destined to have these experiences. They are enigmatic but -luckily for us --those who recorded the story in the gospels kept the mystery in the words, and did not try to explain them in detail. Many will deny it, but they are not lost because of their denial, for nothing is lost but the son of perdition -the belief in destruction and death.

Everyone, seeing their friends depart this world have to admit to themselves that things do die. We came down into a world where everything dies; yet I tell you: nothing really dies, but returns by the seed of contemplative thought. But that is not the mystery of Christmas.

I tell you: God himself is housed in that which appears to die. He is dreaming this dream of death which we call life. One day he will awaken through a definite series of events, beginning with his resurrection. Blake claims the sleep of death is 6,000 years. I do not know how long my dream was, but I do know that when I awoke it seemed as though I had been there for an eternity.

My skull was completely sealed, but I had an innate knowledge as to what to do. I pushed the base of my skull and something gave, leaving a hole which I squeezed myself through and came out of that skull, just like a child comes out of its mother's womb.

Then the imagery of scripture, as told in the 2nd chapter of the Book of Luke, surrounded me. I held the sign -the little child wrapped in swaddling clothes -in my arms and saw the three witnesses to the event, those who were told to "Go quickly into Bethlehem where you will find a sign that a Savior was born this day."

God is the savior of the world as told us in the 43rd and 45th chapters of the Book of Isaiah. "I am the Lord your God, the Holy One of Israel, your Savior and besides me there is no savior." The savior's name is I am.

It is God who awoke when I awoke in my skull. In the Book of Psalms, God is told to "Rouse thyself, why sleepest thou, O Lord." It is God who sleeps and dreams the dream of life, animating the world of death until he awakes within the skull of man where he first entered. His departure from that tomb is the birth we now celebrate on the 25th day of December.

This is followed by the great revelation of remembrance, for on that day God's son David reveals your fatherhood. After this revelation you will understand the words of Robert Grave's poem which I have quoted, because only then will you know true unity. If I am the father of your son, and one you know other than the speaker is the father of our son, are we not one father? So in the end there is only one body, one Lord, one Spirit, one God and Father of all.

One body fell. Its fragmentation is humanity. We are all sons of God being collected and brought back into the true unity as God the Father.

Having played all the parts -the good, the bad and the indifferent -your son reveals your fatherhood. When these signs confront you, your journey is at its end.

Christianity is based upon the affirmation that a series of events happened in which God revealed himself in action for the salvation of his sons. God brings all the sons back by giving them himself; and it takes all the sons to form God, so in the end there is only God the Father.

It takes one who has experienced scripture to explain it. Who would have believed the third chapter of John could be literally true? Calling himself the son of man he said: "As Moses lifted up the serpent in the wilderness, so must the son of man be lifted up."

I know this truth from experience for I -a son of man -was lifted up in spiral form, just like a fiery serpent, right into the kingdom of heaven - which is within, as told us in the Book of Luke. As the temple of the Living God, my body split from top to bottom, and I -the son of man - rose into that heavenly state like a serpent, as it reverberated like thunder.

And who would have thought that when the Holy Spirit descends, it is in the bodily form of a dove, but it is. The Holy Spirit so loves you because you have finished the work that you, yourself, set out to do, that he penetrates the ring of offense to demonstrate his love.

We, a brotherhood of one, agreed to dream in concert before we descended and became fragmented. In this world we are seemingly separate brings, at war with one another, and yet there is no other because eventually we will be the Father of God's only son. So,

"Hold fast with both hands To that Royal Love which alone As we know certainly, Restores fragmentation into true unity."

Here is one who stands before you and speaks of being here, yet tells you that he is to come. Then he asks the question: "Will he find faith upon the earth?' So he is always coming, always awakening, and one in whom he awakens turns to his immediate circle and wonders if anyone will believe him.

In the story, Jesus is a wine bibber, a glutton, a man of the world who loves harlots and tax collectors and all the sinners. He has awakened in me, and because I, too, like a good dinner, a good bottle of wine, and a few good martinis, my testimony is dismissed; and I am considered an impostor, because this is not a popular concept of what Jesus ought to be.

But I say to you, if anyone tells you: "Come, I have found him," do not go, because God cannot be found any place but within you. He is buried in you, will awaken in you, and rise in you, as you.

"It does not yet appear what we shall be, but we know that when he appears we shall be like him." Have you seen his face? It is just like yours, but raised to the nth degree of perfection. He is the Rock, and the Rock is

Christ. We have forgotten the Rock that begot us, and are unmindful of the Rock that gave us birth.

That Rock was fragmented, and you forgot that the world round about you was nothing more than yourself pushed out. So you have fought shadows, believing in the seeming other, when housed within that seeming other is the only God, and you are he. The same series of events will awaken in him as they will in you, and in the end we will all know each other.

Even though I know I am God the Father, and you know that you are God the Father, there is no loss of identity. And for all the identity of person, there is this strange, peculiar discontinuity of earthly form. You will wear your earthly face, raised to the nth degree of perfection. You will have a human voice and hands, but your body is indescribable. It is wisdom and above all things, it is Love.

Everyone in the universe will experience the mystery we are now about to celebrate, called Christmas. This is not some little day that took place once and for all 2,000 years ago. It is always taking place, for it is the coming of God, awakening within man. Were he not in you, you could not breathe. So he slays the son of perdition by the breath of his mouth, and destroys him by his appearing and his coming.

God the Father is within you, emanating the garment you are wearing. He cleaves to it, and you -in turn cleave to him, until one day you learn to love only one being, and see that one being reflected in all things.

Hold to him. His name is I am. He loves his emanation and will cleave to him and they will become one. Then he awakes, wearing that individualized face which is perfect. I will meet you in eternity and I will know you; but for all the identity of person, there will be a discontinuity of form. A form that is glorious beyond the wildest dream of man. The form is all power, all wisdom, and all love. We purposely descended into this world to accomplish that end.

I hope that when you get together on Christmas day to celebrate with your family and friends, that you will remember what Christmas really means, and know that everyone present will have this experience.

They, too, will awaken to being God the Father. This I know, and because there is only one Father, he is one with the world. All the brothers will return, and in returning they will be God the Father; for it was God's pleasure and will to give himself to all of his sons, so when all return, they are God Himself.

Now let us go into the silence.

The Secret *of* Causation

"The secret of imagining is the greatest of all problems, to the solution of which every man should aspire; for supreme power, supreme wisdom, and supreme delight, lie in the solution of this great mystery." Imagination is the Jesus Christ of scripture, and when you solve the great mystery of imagining, you will have found the cause of the phenomena of life. Imagination is called "Jehovah" in the Old Testament and "Jesus" in the New, but they are one and the same being. Divine Imagination, containing all, reproduces itself in the human imagination; therefore, all things exist in the human imagination. When you solve the problem of imagining, you will have found Jesus Christ, the secret of causation.

Let me share with you two experiences which came to me this past week. The first lady said: "Returning from a wonderful cruise recently, I checked my baggage at La Guardia Airport, bound for Chicago, where I expected to spend a few days with friends. Arriving in Chicago, I discovered that the bag which contained most of my clothes and all of the presents I had bought for my friends and relatives -as well as a locket I had had made from the engagement and wedding band my late husband had given me -was missing. I immediately reported the loss to the airline, but when I arrived in California there was still no trace of it.

"A week later I received a letter saying that the bag could not be located, and my first reaction was to curse the airline for their negligence; but then I remembered that imagining creates reality. I tried to reconstruct the letter, but when I couldn't feel its words were true, I began to assume that the bag had arrived at the house. I lifted it up on the bed, opened it, put my clothes away, as well as the gifts which were there. I did this every night and during the day, when I would notice my thoughts going astray.

"When the grandchildren would ask about their presents, I told them that they were on their way, as I never admitted to anyone that the bag was lost. How could I, if I believe what I had imagined? Six weeks later I received a letter from the airline saying: `If you do not pick up your bag within five days, you will be charged storage.' I picked up the bag to find everything there, and put them all away, just as I had imagined doing." Then the lady added this thought: "Love's labor is never lost. Everything in that bag was loved, and I knew that if this principle was true, it would prove itself in the testing -and it did."

I can't thank her enough for sharing this experience with me, that I, in turn, may share it with you. Everything is created by the human imagination. There is no other God. You can use your imagination wisely and create a heaven here on earth, or use it foolishly and create the world's havoc; but there is only one power, called the Lord God Jehovah in the Old Testament, and Jesus Christ in the New.

This lady's first impulse was to curse the person who stupidly lost the bag. Then, remembering what she had heard, she tried to revise the letter. When that didn't seem natural, she asked herself what she would do if the bag was now in her possession. Assuming it was there, she did everything she would do if it was a physical fact -and six weeks later it was.

That is what I mean by imagining creating reality, for an assumption is faith; and without faith it is impossible to please your own wonderful human imagination. Divine Imagination, containing all, reproduces itself in human imagination; therefore, the human imagination contains all. The world is the human imagination pushed out. Not knowing this, man cheats himself, murders himself, declares war against himself, and does all sorts of evil against himself; but do not let yourself be intimidated by the horror of the world. Leave it alone, for it is only the misuse of the power exercised by sleeping mankind.

Now, another lady shared this experience with me: She found herself in a neighbor's kitchen, filled with men and women dressed as Mennonites. (You all know what the Mennonite look like. Originating in Zurich, Switzerland in the year 1525, they moved into Germany, France, Belgium, and Holland, to finally arrive in this country in the 17th century. Now numbering around 150,000 to 200,000, they continue to dress and live in the same fashion they did when they arrived here 300 years ago. Here is a fixed belief which has perpetuated itself year after year.)

The neighbor's second husband had mistreated her, so the Mennonites killed him. Although she tried to tell them that it was wrong to take the life of another, as far as they were concerned it was the right thing to do. He had joined their society and knew their laws, which stated that if a man mistreated a woman, he was to be killed. No matter what argument she used, she could not persuade them that what they had done was wrong.

In the 16th chapter of the Book of Proverbs you will read: "All the ways of a man are pure in his own eyes, but God weighs the heart. God has made everything for its purpose, even the wicked for the day of trouble." Believing in an eye for an eye and a tooth for a tooth, they felt no remorse or guilt for their actions, for in their eyes it was perfect.

Suddenly a limousine appeared and men dressed in black and carrying machine guns entered the house. As she watched, the leader, pointing his gun at the lady, ordered the others to search the house. Then the lady awoke, not to find herself on her bed, but standing in the room of her dream. Suddenly realizing that she was awake in her dream and the action was taking place within her, she stopped the activity, which allowed her to see anyone as alive and independent of her perception, and they all froze.

(As Blake said, "All that you behold, though it appears without, it is within, in your human imagination of which this world of mortality is but a shadow.")

Turning to the leader she said: "You don't want to kill her, you love her and she loves you." Then turning to the woman she said, "You love him and he loves you." Allowing them to obey her will, she stood back and watched, as the man put his gun down and -with outstretched arms - moved to embrace the woman. Turning to go into the kitchen and release the animation there, her alarm caused her to awaken to this level of her dream.

This world is just as much a dream as that one, but man is sound asleep and does not know that he is dreaming. No one will sentence a man for dreaming he killed another; rather they will try to analyze it for him, and most of our so-called experts on dreams are past masters of misinterpretation. They do not realize the great mystery surrounding us. I tell you: the whole vast world is the individual dreamer pushed out, and the conflict is within himself, and not on the outside.

This lady's drama began as something taking place on the outside, and seemingly independent of her perception of it. Then she awoke to an activity within her, which was animating and making alive all that she perceived. Arresting it, everyone became frozen, like statues. She changed their intentions, then watched as they were reanimated once more -but now bewildered, because of the radical change in them which took place in her.

Scripture calls this repentance, or metanoia, which means "a radical change of mind." When ideas change, so do your intentions and attitude towards life. The story is told, that at his trial, the Risen Christ said to the symbol of the authority of this world: "You have no power over me, were it not given you from above." This world is a drama which has been set in motion based upon your attitude from above. Functioning from above, this lady is tasting of the power of the age to come.

In the 10th chapter of Luke, the story is told of seventy disciples, who -having been sent out into the world returned thrilled beyond measure, and said: "Lord, even the demons were subject to us in your name." Then he said: "I saw Satan fall from heaven. Nevertheless, rejoice not that the spirits are subject to you, but that your names are written in heaven." I say to her, rejoice not that you have tasted of this power, but rejoice because your name is written in heaven. This is infinitely greater than demonstrating your power in this world.

Now, Luke does not speak of seventy individuals which were sent out, but the numerical value of the Hebrew letter ayin,[1] whose symbolic value is the eye. This is not the outside eye, but the incurrent eye, which sees inward into the world of thought. You have the incurrent eye, nevertheless rejoice — not because the spirit was subject unto you, but because your name is written in heaven. One day when you are called into that assemblage, you will see that there is such a record, and your name is written in heaven.

This may seem stupid to the intelligent mind. That is because they are sound asleep. This Manson boy, now on trial for the murders recently committed by his group, fell into a power of which he is totally unaware. Many who became his slaves were simple people, some cultured. One had attended college for three years.

His power, exercised without love, resulted in a horrible experience; but she exercised her power in love, saying: "You don't want to kill her. You love her and she loves you." She released the man from his violent state by the power of love. This world is every bit as much a dream as that world, and you, its dreamer, are God learning to exercise your powerful imagination, in love.

You can take this message on either level. Use it as my friend did, when she would not accept the fact that her luggage was missing, or test your power from above. Scripture claims that: Whatever you desire, if you will believe you already have it, you will.

Refusing to believe her luggage was missing, my friend fulfilled her desire by placing it on the bed, removing its contents, and putting them away. This she did every night for five weeks, and then one day she received a notice saying that if she did not pick up her luggage within five days she would be charged storage!

I can't thank her enough for sharing this experience with me, that I may share it with you to encourage you to control your human imagination; for if you would steer a true course toward a certain goal in life, you must ever be aware of the end that you are shaping by your imaginal activity, and not allow doubt to enter for one moment. When you know what you want, you must think from your belief in its possession, morning, noon, and night. If you do, no power can stop its appearance, because you are the dreamer of your dream, pushing yourself out, shaping your world by your imaginal activities.

---

[1]

Your own wonderful human imagination is the Jehovah and Jesus of scripture. The words mean: "Jehovah is salvation, or Jehovah saves." In the 3rd chapter of Exodus, Jehovah revealed his name as I am. You are not John or Mary, but simply I am. In the 4th chapter of the Book of Genesis we are told that when Abel (the 2nd son) was killed, Eve bore Seth, a son to take Abel's place. Seth then had a son called Enosh, "And from that day on, men began to call upon the name of God." (Remember, in the lady's dream the second husband was killed.)

Now, the words "call upon" literally mean "call with." It is nonsense to say: "In the name of Jesus; in the name of God; or in the name of Jehovah." If you say: "In the name of Jesus Christ," you do not feel anything. But when you call with the name, you say: I am unpacking the suitcase. I am hanging the clothes in the closet. I am putting the presents away. I am arresting the activity within and silencing those who stand before me. I am saying: "You love her and she loves you.'" That's calling with the name of God. And from that moment on, men began to call with the name of God.

If you really believe me, you will prove my words in the testing. The two ladies have proved it and shared their experiences with me. I can't tell you my thrill when I know that you have heard me to the point of applying my words. One who is the incurrent eyewitness took it into the depth and saw into eternity. The other knows the truth, and believes it on this level of her being. From this level she brought her luggage back with all of its contents in place, while the other went into a deeper level of her being to discover that there was nothing on the outside but herself.

Mennonites are only expressions of fixations. They haven't changed their outer dress in 300 years. Satisfying their conscience, they will loan you a dollar and not accept any interest on the loan; but they can feel justified in buying land and holding it until the price goes up. You see, man has a peculiar, innate something that justifies everything he does, thereby making him pure in his own eyes.

But I say to you: your imagination manifests itself in the imaginations of men. The world is playing its part, because you are imagining every moment in time. Who knows who is treading in the winepress tonight, causing the subtle change in the minds of men. Perhaps he feels wrongfully accused, and is now sitting in jail thinking of getting even with society. That's treading in the winepress. When he can lift his thoughts to the point of vision, the act is committed, and it will manifest itself in the world of man,

Vision is simply awakening in the dream. Asleep, you seem to be the victim of your dreams; but awake, as you are here, you can become discriminating. She awoke in her dream, making it vision. Realizing that it started as a dream -therefore, it must still be a dream -she knew the people were only herself made visible, so she could change them. Placing the thought of love in the mind of the man, he became aware of his radical change of thinking, yet was totally unaware of who produced it.

Who knows who is producing the changes in the minds of men today, producing war or peace. It could be some woman treading in the winepress; or -as Yeats said -it could be in the mind of some shepherd boy, lighting up his eyes for a moment before he ran upon his way. Dreaming of heroism, of noble battles where he was the hero, that little boy can cause the blood to flow. If you know who you are and how imagination operates, you will learn to control your imaginal activities. If you do not, they will be controlled for you by another, and you will become their victim.

Any time you exercise your imagination lovingly on behalf of another you have done the right thing. But if it is not done in love there is a question mark, for God is love. This knowledge is not the result of some philosophic reasoning, but of self-revelation. God unveiled himself within me and now I know that God is Infinite love. Yes, he is Infinite Power and Wisdom as well, but power without love can raise horror.

I say to everyone, believe me. The Jesus of scripture and the Jehovah of scripture are your own wonderful human imagination. There is no other God, and God is love. One day you will know this truth, but in the meanwhile believe me as the lady did. When her natural human impulse was to curse, she blessed by imagining her luggage on her bed. Then she performed in her imagination what she would do in the flesh if her desire was now out-pictured on her screen of space. This world is a play, peopled by those in costumes. You are its author, writing your play. You can change it (as my friend did) and prove to yourself that you can take a fixed idea (symbolized as a Mennonite) and change it.

Believe me, imagining does create reality. Take me seriously. You will never know Jesus until you know the secret of imagining, for your imagination is he. If you really believe in God, believe in your own imagination, for it is the power of God and the wisdom of God. The power and wisdom of the lady's imaginal act influenced the entire outer world and produced that so-called "lost" bag and returned it.

I tell you, there is only one power in the universe. We call it by the name of God or Jesus. But if you think of Jesus as someone on the outside, who lived 2,000 years ago, you will never know him. Nor will you ever know God, if you think of him as some impersonal force. God is a person because you are a person. He became you, as he became us all, that we may become as He is.

Take my message to heart and apply it from now on. You can be the man you would like to be. Don't start dreaming about it. Awake and think from it. Do not concern yourself about trying to meet the so-called "right" people. They are simply reflections of the activity you have placed within you. Change your thoughts and you will change the behavior of those who surround you for they are nothing more than yourself made visible.

The day will come when you will awake from this dream, and you will see what my friend saw in another aspect of the dream -that the world is dead, and only the reflection of an activity of the human imagination. Then you will depart, leaving the world as it is for others to play upon, while you return to the being you really are -the Lord God Himself, the creator of the dream.

Now let us go into the silence.

The Law

The whole vast world is no more than man's imagining pushed out. I must qualify that by saying that the world outside of man is dead, but Man is a living soul, and it responds to man, yet man is sound asleep and does not know it. The Lord God placed man in a profound sleep, and as he sleeps the world responds as in a dream, for Man does not know he is asleep, and then he moves from a state of sleep where he is only a living soul to an awakened state where he is a life-giving Spirit. And now he can himself create, for everything is responding to an activity in man which is Imagination. "The eternal body of man is all imagination; that is God himself."[2]

Three wonderful case histories were given to me last Tuesday and I can best describe what I mean by telling you of one of them. Here is this lady driving east on Sunset and she comes to a stop at Laurel Canyon. A bus is to her right, and then she sees this little elderly lady in grey who is running diagonally across the street through traffic, trying to catch that bus. The bus driver sees her but he pulls out leaving her on the street. The lady, who gave me this story, told me that she felt compassion for this elderly lady, but she was not in a lane where she could give her a lift; she had to pull out with her line when the light changed. She said to herself, "I will give that lady a lift just the same." So in Imagination, she opens her car door and lets her in.

Then still in her Imagination, she hears the lady tell her that she is meeting some friends a few blocks away and if she had to wait for another bus she is afraid they would not wait for her. The lady in the car carried on this imaginary conversation and it took maybe a half a minute until she felt satisfied about it. Four blocks ahead, as she again stopped for a light, someone tapped on the car window, and here stands a breathless little elderly with gray hair dressed in gray. My friend lowered the window and the little lady said "I have missed my bus. Can you give me a lift? Friends are waiting for me and when they see I do not get off the bus they may go on and leave me." My friend let her get into the car and then six blocks

---

[2] Blake

further the little lady said. "There are my friends!" and thanks the driver and gets out.

Now here is a lady whom I say is awake. And may I tell you that in Heaven there was joy because one called a sinner (we are all sinners, for we are all missing the mark, and the mark is to awaken) has discovered that the whole world is responsive to what we are thinking. She could not actually give the first little lady a lift so she did it in Imagination, and then she sees this other elderly lady and gives her a lift. Here she is enacting her imaginary drama, and four blocks later when the dream is completed this little ole lady taps at her car window. In her imagination she gave a lift to a little grey haired lady dressed in gray. Does it matter if it was the lady behind at the last bus stop or this lady dressed in gray? Everyone is responding to what we are doing in our Imagination. There is no outside world that is really alive. It depends, for its aliveness, on the activity of man who is a living soul. Man named the animals, the birds, the trees, – everything. God became man as a living soul, but He had to forget He was God to become man, and now man has to become a life-giving spirit, where he knows that everything is an imaginal activity.

Here, at that corner where the first part of this little drama took place, half of those who witnessed it would bawl out the bus driver for not waiting for the old lady, and the other half would say she was a fool for running into the street. This lady in the car could have reacted like that, for the dreamer does not know that he is dreaming. It is only when we awake they know they are causing the dream, or even had a dream. The lady in the car saw only someone who had failed to realize an objective, so she enacted a scene for her, implying she had realized it. And four blocks later she meets a little old lady who says to her the exact words she had heard in her Imagination. Her Imaginary dream unfolds in detail. An awakened dream is crystallized in the world. "Real are the dreams of gods, as they slowly pass their pleasure in a long immortal dream." When man completely awakens he dreams his pleasure and everything responds while he dreams it.

We think everything in the world is completely independent from our perception of it, but the whole thing is dead. I see it, and come upon it, but the whole thing is dead.... frozen. Then I start an activity within me and then the world that was dead becomes alive, but not knowing I am doing it, I am sound asleep and then the whole thing takes over and it becomes a nightmare. But I must keep control and know it is dependent on me. The world is infinite response and the thing that makes it alive is the living soul called generic man (male-female). And then God wove Himself into the brain of this generic man, and then He sleeps. As man begins to awaken he controls and takes over, and is no longer a victim of his vision, so he has control of his attention. Everyone is free to create his world as he wants it – if he knows that the whole thing is responding to him.

In Luke 13 we are told the story of five Galileans who have been murdered by Pilate. "And he mixed their blood with their offering, etc." And the central figure of the gospels which is your awakened Imagination says to his followers; "Do you think these five were worse sinners than the others? I tell you 'No'. But unless you repent you will all likewise perish in the same manner." Here on one level we think it served them right, just as those who saw the scene on the Sunset Blvd. would say "It served her right – cutting across the street like that!" In this story in Luke we are told that a man sinned in the past and was murdered by Pilate. It has nothing to do with it. Then Jesus asked them, "Do you think that the eighteen upon whom the tower in Siloam fell and killed them were worse offenders than the others who dwell in Jerusalem? I tell you, No; but unless you repent you will all likewise perish.

On this level of the dream people think of getting even. It is a dream of confusion and people are reactivating, but man has to awaken and become an actor. On this present level man is always reflecting life, not knowing he is the cause of all he observes. But when he awakens from the dream and then becomes an actor. What percentage would have done what this lady in the car did? They would have reacted, or feasted on the fruit of the tree of good and evil. They would have had a violent reaction, and then they would have had a violent resistance from this dead universe. But this lady makes her dream and the whole thing comes to pass exactly as she pictured it, even to the number of blocks. You might almost think she had manufactured that little old lady in gray, but I tell you everything comes in response to our own wonderful imaginal activity.

You can be anything in this world but you cannot know it or expect it to come unless you Act. If you react based on the past, you continue in the same pattern. To be the man you desire to be you must create the scene, as this lady did, and the whole world will be convulsed if that is necessary to bring it to pass. There is no other power but God, but God had to "forget" he was God in this state of sleep, and then He awakens and consciously determines the conditions he wants in the world.

So again I say to this lady, the angels rejoiced over your awakening, and – I say this without pride – they also rejoiced because I kept my promise that I would come and awaken this sleeper in the world of men. For I, also, had to forget everything to become man. For when one goes and then returns he has to forget everything to become man. For when one goes, and then returns he has to forget everything, but he promises he will carry out his pledge and help man awaken. Then the living soul becomes a life-giving spirit, and then creates.

Take it seriously. Do not go through this with your dream un-acted. It took this lady 30 seconds to enact her drama and another 60 seconds to realize it. You tell yourselves -it must take time-What time? Read Corinthians 1:18, I could go before men with all the words of wisdom, but know only one thing, the cross. To the wise it is foolishness, etc. What is the cross? Think of it in this light. You began, seemingly in your mother's womb and end in the grave. You do not, but you have that picture. Look on the horizontal line of the cross as time. Intersecting this vertical line and call that infinite states, like Jacobs ladder. At any section of time I can move up or down. Time is flowing and the state with which I am identified still unfolds.

So, while seated in my car I can move up and enact a drama. I acted and remained within that state. It unfolded. It took 60 seconds. There are infinite states intersecting the line of time. We become one with a certain state and it demonstrates itself in actual phenomena. Everyone here, it need not take you more than 30 seconds to bring about a change of state. What would it be like? And you name your desire. Remain in that state, and that state, by the passage of time, will unfold in your world. You do nothing about it once you have entered the state…for the outer must move by compulsion of the inner power.

This little lady in gray had to come to my friend's car. Every detail of that imaginary act took place.

Why not? The universe is infinite response. When you know that there is no one in the whole world could ever faze you, because he is a shadow. I have seen the whole world dead, completely frozen, and then I allowed something within me to start and everything became animated. Then you ask yourself a million questions. Who am I? What is it all about? Why? Everything here is responding to the imaginal activity within man.

When someone who is sick becomes well: when someone who is blind then sees, is that more of a miracle than what this lady told? She is awake. If you make a fortune it means nothing. All the honors of men in a state of sleep are as nothing. You must "repent". It has nothing to do with the so-called judgment of God. It is only a dream and man is reacting to the dream and he does not know that he is the dreamer and causing all the dream.

The literal meaning of the Greek word translated as repent means "a change of mind." It has nothing to do with the moral picture. The churches introduced that, but it has nothing to do with it. I don't care what a man has done, if he changes his mind in this meaning of the word "repent" things will change, for he is then on the line of vertical line of states. He stands at a point on the states. There are infinite states and we must learn to distinguish between the state and the individual occupying the state. But I can now change and move into another state. I can in Time, do it in a split second and rise on the vertical line of the states.

So, "I come, only to teach the cross.", said Paul. I will rise within myself and ignore the former state, and within myself I will assume that things are as I want them to be. If I remain faithful, the passage of Time will unfold it. So, Blake said, "Eternity is in love with the productions of Time." I tell you, do not let anyone ever convince you that because of your past accomplishments or your present state in the world that you cannot change your position by rising within yourself, and then see the whole world respond. And I mean NOW!

So, I tell you this lady is awake; the Child is awake in her, the purpose of life is to awake. If the whole vast world or sleeping humanity thought her important, would she feel flattered? If in a dream everyone praised you and then you awoke and found it was all a dream, would you be flattered? One dreamer puts a medal on another dreamer, and they do not know it. It is only the awakening that is important. Awakening and doing the will of God. God's will is in you active as your own Imagination, and His will is to realize the imaginal state. To realize something novel as this lady did or to maintain something to maintain in being, or to let things go that you feel are unlovely. I will do it all and only act, and stop re-acting. Then the whole book, The Bible, becomes alive. Leave all the "wise men to mock it or tolerate". Let them reach the moon or the stars, they are all dead. Nothing lives outside of man. Man is the living soul, turning slowly into a life-giving Spirit. But you cannot tell it except in a parable or metaphor to excite the mind of man to get him to go out and prove it.

Leave the good and evil and eat of the Tree of Life. Nothing in the world is untrue if you want it to be true. You are the truth of everything that you perceive. "I am the truth, and the way, the life revealed." If I have physically nothing in my pocket, then in Imagination I have MUCH. But that is a lie based on fact, but truth is based on the intensity of my imagination and then I will create it in my world. Should I accept facts and use them as to what I should imagine? No.

It is told us in the story of the fig tree. It did not bear for three years. One said, "Cut it down, and throw it away." But the keeper of the vineyard pleaded NO"! Who is the tree? I am the tree; you are the tree. We bear or we do not. But the Keeper said he would dig around the tree and feed it – or manure it, as we would say today – and see if it will not bear. Well I do that here every week and try to get the tree – you – me to bear. You should bear whatever you desire. If you want to be happily married, you should be. The world is only response. If you want money, get it. Everything is a dream anyway. When you awake and know what you are creating and that you are creating it that is a different thing.

The greatest book is the Bible, but it has been taken from a moral basis and it is all weeping and tears. It seems almost ruthless as given to us in the Gospel, if taken literally. The New Testament interprets the Old Testament, and it has nothing to do with morals. You change your mind and stay in that changed state until it unfolds. Man thinks he has to work himself out of something, but it is God asleep in you as a living soul, and then we are reborn as a life-giving spirit. We do it here in this little classroom called Earth or beyond the grave, for you cannot die. You can be just as asleep beyond the grave. I meet them constantly, and they are just like this. Same loves and same hates. No change. They will go through it until they finally awake, until they cease to re-act and begin to act.

Do not take this story lightly which I have told you tonight. Take it to heart. Tonight when you are driving home enact a scene. No matter what it is. Forget good and evil. Enact a scene that implies you have what you desire, and to the degree that you are faithful to that state, it will unfold in your world and no power can stop it, for there is no other power.

Nothing is independent of your perception of it, and this goes for that great philosopher among us who is still claiming that everything is independent of the perceiver, but that the perceiver has certain powers. It is not so. Nothing is independent of the perceiver. Everything is "burned up" when I cease to behold it. It may exist for another, but not for me.

Let us make our dream a noble one, for the world is infinite response to you, the being you want to be.

Now let us go into the silence.

Power Called "The Law"

Any presentation of a doctrine must show that it has specific reference to life now, as well as hereafter, for secularized man is far more concerned with the present than with the future. So, if you would interest anyone in the truth, you must first appeal to the power they can experience here and now; for the promise is so fantastic that if they heard it first they might turn away in disgust. Show them what they can do right here and now. Get their interest in the power called "The Law," and then perhaps they will desire to know of the promise.

Let me share with you now a couple of stories a gentleman shared with me this week. He said: "About ten days ago my wife told me of a little girl only fourteen months old who had developed lumps on her neck [in] which - when the doctor removed and tested a lump - there were signs of cancer. Three specialists had been brought in and each separately had declared the child had cancer. Only one doctor, looking at the results questioned the verdict, but they were keeping the child in the hospital for further examination. As I listened to her story I cued my wife's voice out to the point that I couldn't even hear what she was saying, but hearing her voice, I reconstructed the story and heard its revision in my mind's eye. That night as I fell asleep I listened again and heard my wife tell me the revised story. A few days later the doctors made another test from another lump and the vote was unanimous, the child did not have cancer. And since they had performed no remedial treatment in the hospital, they determined she never did have cancer, for without treatment the child could not have overcome the condition. When my wife heard the new verdict she told the grandmother and the mother what I had done, but they could not believe that an imaginal act has any power of causation."

To the world it is the height of insanity to believe that imagining creates reality, yet every mystic knows that every natural effect has a spiritual cause. A natural cause only seems to be. It is a delusion of this world, as man's memory is so poor he cannot relate what is taking place now to a former imaginal act. Always looking for physical causation, man cannot believe he imagined anything that could have produced such a physical effect; yet I tell you: as you sit alone and imagine you are setting a cause in motion, and when you see its effects you may deny the imaginal state, but your "now" is alive and real to you because of an imaginal act on your part and for no other reason. Your imagination sets everything in motion, but your memory is faulty; therefore you may look upon one who claims life is caused by imagination as a fool - yet Blake would call you an idiot reasoner, not a man of imagination. Now, my friend continued, saying: "Driving home from work the other night I was thinking I could use a little more cash, as Uncle Sam would be making demands upon my income. Then I began to imagine lovely, green, crisp currency raining down on me. For about one minute I lost myself in a little shower of green currency. Then the traffic demanded my attention and I assumed my normal, alert state and forgot all about my imaginal act until the morning of the fifteenth of April. At that time my boss entered the office and said: `You will receive a ten per cent raise in salary retroactive to April first,' and handed me a check."

Now, let me warn you tonight, wait until you get home to try it. It's much better to imagine the crisp currency falling on your bed than on the freeway! But do it, for I tell you everything is an imaginal act. There is no such thing as physical causation. It's all imaginal, but the world will not accept it. They laugh at the man of imagination but they cannot disprove it. A man may physically strike another. That was the physical cause while the blow he received was the effect; therefore the whole thing appeared to be constructed physically, but I ask you: what preceded the impulse to strike? That impulse was the unseen cause, which was an imaginal act. The world is brought into being by imagination and sustained by imagination, and when imagination no longer sustains it, it dissolves and leaves not a trace behind. One must approach the gospel on this level first. If one's interest is aroused on this level and it is proved to be true in the testing, then they may be interested in hearing about the promise.

Now I go back to the little girl. Judged by human standards the garment she wears is only fourteen months old, but the wearer of that garment is as old as God himself, and God has no beginning and no end. He chose us in him, not when we came out from our mother's womb, but before the foundation of the world. Before physical creation you and I were chosen in him for a purpose, for without purpose what would anything matter if death was final? Many tyrants believe that, and with those kinds of thoughts you cannot blame them for being a tyrant. If you believed death ended it all you would no doubt do as they do. You would agree with Macbeth, when Shakespeare had him say: "It is a tale told by an idiot, full of sound and fury signifying nothing." That's what the world would have to be if there was no promise, no purpose or meaning behind it. But if you can get their interest in the law enough to test it and it proves itself in performance, then you can tell them the greatest story in the world in the hope that they will believe or begin to believe it.

Not a thing said of Jesus can be proved outwardly. He can only be known by the visionaries. While living in this mortal body and known only by the mask I wear, the incredible story called Jesus Christ has unfolded in me. I have taken you, my friends, into my confidence and shared my experiences with you in the hope that you will believe me. You see me as alive and well, yet I know what it is to be crucified, buried, and resurrected. While in my heavenly body I chose one among you to give my immortal eyes that have been turned inward, not outward, that confirmation of my words may come from her. She has seen me nailed on a cross, which was burned to the ground leaving golden, liquid light at its base, just as I told her it had happened to me. No one can persuade her that she did not have that experience, any more than someone could persuade me that I did not have the experience.

Now this lady knows who Jesus is. Knowing me as a man with all of the weaknesses of the flesh and its limitations, she had gone beyond the mask through vision and seen who Jesus really is. He has made known unto me the mystery of his will according to his purpose which he set forth in Christ as a plan for the fullness of time, that he may unite all things in him - things in heaven and things on earth. Jesus is God's plan of salvation which is in you. That plan has erupted in me and I have shared my experiences with you who come here, and also in my book, Resurrection.

Now, only the visionary, only he who has the immortal eyes, will actually know who Jesus is, for he is from above and is not of this world at all. It was he who said: "You are from below and I am from above. You are of this world and I am not of this world"; yet, throughout history, man has been looking for Jesus in the Near East. Those who have not had the visions claim they know the spot where he was crucified and buried, the road he walked, and even claim to have a little piece of wood from the cross upon which he was nailed. They perpetuate a tradition, making void the word of God as told us in the 15th chapter of Matthew. Keeping the traditions of a physical Jesus alive, the truth has been made void, as Jesus is not a physical being but a pattern buried in every one. When this pattern erupted in me, I was as surprised as anyone could be, and although I still remain in this weak little garment of flesh and continue to suffer through all the temptations of the world, I cannot deny my visions.

Now I have given my immortal eyes to one who in turn gave them to another, who will in turn give them to another, that they may all become eyewitnesses, as Luke speaks of in the beginning of his story, saying: "Inasmuch as many have undertaken to compile a narrative of the things which have been accomplished among us, just as they were presented to us by those who from the beginning were eyewitnesses..." Then he added this thought: "...and ministers of the word, it seemed good to me also, to write a narrative, most excellent Theophilus, concerning the things which have been accomplished among us." Luke was able to tell all who loved God (called Theophilus) the truth because of the eyewitnesses. But when the eyewitnesses depart this world the ministers multiply. They are men without vision who never knew the one who, while walking in the flesh, gave his eyes to those who bore witness to his story. Having witnessed the drama as it unfolded within him, they depart this world and leave only the ministers of the word, who build organizations and make a little god out of the man who - while like all other men - experienced God's plan of salvation in him. They say nothing of the pattern's eruption, but only of the external man - when there is no external Jesus.

You could look from now until the end of time and never find any convincing evidence of the historicity of one called Jesus - yet he is real. He is your true being, your hope of glory. Do you not realize that Jesus Christ is in you? Unless, of course, you fail to meet the test. Test him on his level. Test your creative power, called the law. Imitate my friend and allow a gentle shower of currency to fall upon you. Believe you have received them and you will. Then share your knowledge with others and show them that scripture has a specific reference to life, now! Do not start with the hereafter. You can tell them of the promise later. And remember: nothing is impossible to imagination and the world is created in the imagination.

As a reasoning being you are not responsible to make anything happen. But as a man of imagination you simply imagine it is! My friend knows nothing about cancer. If he saw a cancer cell under a microscope he wouldn't recognize it. He is not a doctor and knows no more about the human body than I do, but he does know what his wife would tell him if the verdict was reversed and the child was well. When his wife told her friend of her husband's imaginal act, the friend (as the world) dismissed the idea, for she could not believe that causation was mental. To her everything has a physical cause and must be cured physically, yet I tell you: life itself is an imaginal journey. My friend heard his wife tell him of the child and then, knowing what he wanted to hear, he changed her words in his imagination. That is all he did. And those words could not return unto him void, but had to accomplish that which he purposed on the inside. He did nothing on the outside to bring it to pass. He simply remained faithful to his imaginal act and it was fulfilled.

I ask you to try it, and then turn to your neighbors and say: "Did it ever occur to you that your world is caused - not by the obvious, but by an unseen imaginal act?" You may interest them that way and if you do, ask them to try it. If they do, and it comes to pass then you can present them with the promise. You can tell them how their weak little garment is transformed as they rise from the dead into life everlasting. I tell you: you will be a completely transformed being with a human face, human hands and voice; but the form you wear cannot be described other than light.

The one thing that separates man from all other creation is his hand. The monkey doesn't have a hand. It cannot fashion, but with a hand you can become a builder. The first word in the name YOD HEY VAV HEY means "hand." It is the hand of the creator that fashions. If you could not fashion a suit of clothes for your body you would have to go nude, but given a hand you can turn yourself into the Father's image, which is a fiery being that you will awaken and know yourself to be.

The majority of the people you speak to will not listen to you. They would rather remain the same little being they know themselves to be and to continue to wear a garment of flesh and blood which must be taken to the bathroom several times a day to perform its normal functions. Can you imagine the hell you would experience if restoration were perpetuated forever? But this is not the body you wear when you know yourself to be God. It is entirely different. It is a heavenly body - a body of fire and air that you are destined to awaken as, for that is the one body we will all know ourselves to be. But while you are here, don't neglect the law. Use it every moment of time. Nothing is beyond your ability to imagine it. You are not responsible for making it so, you simply imagine it is so and let it be so! That is how the world in which we live came into being.

Before you judge me I ask you to test my words. It would be foolish to pass judgment on something you haven't tested. I have known those who claim they do not like something even though they have never tried it, but I tell you: you can acquire a taste for anything. I remember the first time I had an oyster. I was about eleven years old when mother and I visited the little island of St. Croix. In those days there were no hotels, only rooming houses and we all sat at the same common table. Everyone there spoke Danish and I couldn't understand one word they were saying, so I watched and did as they were doing. On the plate before me sat a dish with six little things in shells placed on it. Since I had never seen anything like it before, I watched the hostess. She picked up a little fork, stuck it into one of the things, and as she placed it in her mouth her face burst into a wonderful smile. Expecting the same thing, I picked up my fork, stuck it in the thing and put it in my mouth. Well, it wouldn't go down and I couldn't spit it out. Paralyzed, I realized that if I died in the attempt I had to swallow that thing, and when I did I looked down and turned green as I realized I had five more to go. But I did it, and now I love oysters in any form.

So I say: you can acquire a taste for anything in this world as well as the heavenly world. Start with the law. Learn how it works, and after proving it in performance you may desire to discover who Jesus really is. You may have been taught that a woman called Mary was impregnated by

God and brought forth a physical son who was named Jesus; yet I tell you: I am a normal person, not formerly educated, married, once divorced, with two children - but I have experienced everything said of Jesus Christ in the gospel. And I gave my immortal eyes to a friend (who, married twice, with children from two different men) that she may see me hanging on a cross which was set aflame and reduced to molten, golden liquid light. Seeing the body that sleeps on the bed placed on a pallet, and then on a cross, she has seen the body I wear at night, and now knows who Jesus really is. No, he is not the little garment of flesh you wear, but an eternal pattern of redemption who sleeps in it. He awoke in a garment the world knows as Neville. Having awakened, I know I am He who became humanity that humanity may become God.

God now sleeps in you. He will awake and you will experience the identical drama as recorded in the gospels by one called Jesus Christ, for there is no other and there never will be another being. Those who have been enriched by the law you have taught them may turn from you, because it takes quite a while for traditions to die - as told us in the 15th chapter of the Book of Matthew: "For the sake of your traditions you have made void the word of God." Keeping traditions alive by wearing all these silly little red and purple robes on the outside, the unthinking millions consider themselves blessed if - as he walks by - they touch his garment, or attend a service where the great one is conducting mass. But because of those traditional beliefs the word of God is made void.

I am telling you what I know from experience. Take me seriously, because I must soon depart and those of you with the incurrent eyes will see as I have told you that you would. Then you will depart to leave behind only the ministers, who will turn my experiences into their institutional concept and once again void the word of God.

Tonight use the law and prove its power by becoming the man you imagine yourself to be. But don't forget the promise, for without the promise what would it matter if you owned the earth? I recently read the book Stalin's daughter wrote about her father. In it she told of being present when he died. She said that he was paralyzed on one side, his brain was gone, and he was physically blind; yet he saw something that caused him to raise his good hand and motion with, it as an expression of extreme hate covered his face. It was as though he were defying the devil himself who stood before him. He could have seen a composite picture of the twenty million lives he destroyed, personified as one man, causing his little hand to be raised in defiance as he departed. He didn't believe in life hereafter. He didn't believe he would be restored to life, therefore he felt free to do everything and anything he wanted to. Standing on the balcony watching thousands cheer him, he would say: "Fools!" He saw them as the chaff of life, yet today these trivial people balloon Stalin as an important figure in history. But, he has to face himself now. No longer playing the part of Stalin, the same being is now a young man, healthy and strong, continuing his life, doing something that is consistent with his life to bring out that plan of salvation called Jesus, which - hidden in him - he denied while he was here.

I ask you to use this power called the law. Simply determine what you want and imagine a scene which would imply you have realized it. Enter into the spirit of the scene. Participate in it by giving it sensory vividness. Then relax as you feel its reality. Don't consider the means. Know your desire is already an accomplished fact and you are now reveling in it. Then have faith, for faith is loyalty to your unseen reality. Your imaginal act, although unseen, is reality for God did it. If I asked you who is imagining it, you would respond: "I am" and that is God's name forever and forever.

Learn to live in your imagination morning, noon, and night. This gentleman whose experiences I shared with you tonight told me that when he first heard me he thought I was crazy; but he tried it, and although it didn't make sense it worked. I know the law and the promise do not make sense from a worldly point of view, yet I tell you: there is a plan of redemption buried in you which will erupt in the fullness of time and you will experience all that is said of a man called Jesus in scripture. Then you will know he was never a physical being, but the name of a plan. Jesus is Jehovah, who is your own wonderful I AM.

The root of the Greek word translated "gather" in the expression used in the first chapter of Ephesians is "head." That is where we will all gather together, for that is where we were all crucified and buried. And it is from the head that we resurrect. Returning from this external world, we gather all together into the one state which is in the head. James Dean once said: "The creator of this infinite unity resembles an infinite brain and we but brain cells in the mind of the dreamer." And now the brain cell is expanding within the one brain!

Now let us go into the silence.

Your Supreme Dominion

As you have been told, this morning's subject is "Your Supreme Dominion". As a man does not possess it or he does not know that he possesses it for he certainly is not exercising it. As we read in the very first chapter of the Book of Genesis, "And God made man in His own image, in the image of God made He him. He made them male and female, and God blessed them." And God said unto them, "Be fruitful and multiply and replenish the earth, and subdue it and have dominion over all the fish of the sea and all the fowls of the air, and every moving thing that moves upon the earth. And God saw all that He had done, all that He had done, all that He had made, and they were very good."

Now, you and I reading the Bible, not knowing it to be a psychological truth and seeing it as historical fact, we cannot understand the word. But when man knows the Bible is the greatest collection of psychological truths and was never intended to be seen as history or cosmology, then he gets a glimpse into this great wonderful book. For man himself is the great psychological earth that must be subdued. In man move all the passions, all the great emotions symbolized as creeping things and animals. In the deep of man actually live the invisible states symbolized as fish. In the deep of man actually live all the unnumbered infinite ideas symbolized as the fowls of the air. It is this man that must be self subdued, for subdue it, then comes the promise and have dominion over this vast wonderful country that is man. If man does not know that he himself is the earth spoken of, he thinks he must go out into the world and conquer it. The world reflects the work done on man. And so when he looks upon this wonderful world round about him, he thinks himself so little.

The Bible also tells us he calls himself a grasshopper, and referring to himself as a grasshopper, he sees giants in the land, the giants of industry, the giants of economics, the giants all round about him, and he feels smaller and smaller because he does not know how to go about actually subduing the earth, which is himself. When man knows it, he will realize that man as an individual is supreme within the circle of his own consciousness, for within the circle of his consciousness the entire drama of life is re-enacted over and over again. He has to start with self and then he will see this outer wonderful world, this visible world, is not what he thinks it to be, a place of exile from God; it is the living garment of the Father, and although to many of us its discordant harmony needs some interpretation, to the wise it has a voice and the voice speaks of hidden things behind the veil hidden things behind the veil of man's mind, for this whole vast wonderful world is a response to the arrangement of man's mind. For when he knows it he will look within for the hidden causes, look into the deep to see the fish and how they swim and how they are related, for this arrangement of the deep is going to project itself as circumstances and conditions of life.

And so today, if you haven't started, today is the time to start to really put into practice this teaching, and make of this violence a garden of God. It is called Eden and man was placed within it to keep it and to care it, for the garden of God is man. It is the mind of man. You never find a garden unless a man is present, for without a man there would be a forest of wilderness. But when a man is placed in it he begins to cut the trees or the seeds of wrong thinking; he clears the ground and he cultivates the ground, and then plants wisely. Then you will have dominion, for you will select the seed you will plant, the ideas you will entertain, and you will cultivate them. Knowing the outer world constantly bears witness of the inner arrangement of mind, you will only select the things you want to project into the living garment of your Father. For the whole vast world round about you is a living garment worn by your Father.

So how did he reap? He said He made man in His own image; well, the methods of mental and spiritual knowledge are entirely different. You and I can know a thing mentally by looking at it from the outside, by comparing it with other things, by analyzing it, by defining it, by even giving a description of it, but we can know a thing spiritually only by becoming it. We must be the thing itself if we would know that thing spiritually. We must be in love if we would know love. We must be God like if we would know what God is. For God made me, not out of something other than Himself; He made me perfect, so He made me by becoming me. There was no other way in the world that God could have made me unless He became me. So God became man that He may know man in the only way that He could know anything, for He knows all things spiritually and He calls them very good.

So He made me by becoming me, and now I am called upon to go and take care of the earth, and to subdue it, and take dominion. And I am the earth -I must learn to plant as He planted, and He planted the world by becoming the world. I must now plant as man, by becoming the man I want to be. So I will itemize all the things, name them, give a name to everything I want to express as a man, and then know it spiritually by becoming and I become it as He became me. I identify myself with it and live in that identity and I clothe it in flesh, I clothe it in fact. Not one thing in the world that is mine can be taken from me save by detachment from the state where that thing I love has its natural life. If I live in a world of beauty, if I live in a world of friendship, of comfort and all the lovely things that men enjoy, no power in the world can take one of them from me save I, who live among them, detach myself from the state where these lovely things have their natural life. When you and I know it, we begin to cultivate the earth, we actually weed the mind of all negative states, all unlovely emotions, and we bring into subjection not the outer but the inner, and then the outer reflects that cultivation on self.

Now, how is it done? You are told in the first book of the Bible how it's done. For the promise is to the man who does it and the promise is a complete expansion beyond his wildest dreams of the state he plants. The one who first did it was called Jacob; well, I am Jacob. You are Jacob if you start to plant; every man is the potential Jacob, and Jacob did it by righteousness. As you are told, he did it through righteousness and he multiplied exceedingly, so that he increased a thousand fold his flocks, his cattle; he increased and grew beyond the measure of man in having all the maid servants and men servants and the camels. And this is what he said, "My righteousness shall speak for me in time to come."

Righteousness is right consciousness. The only right consciousness is the consciousness of already being the man you want to be, for that attaches you with an invisible state. You can't see it yet but you become attached to the state that you dare to assume you are, and you go fishing in the deep, you are beginning now to subdue the deep. You enter a state through the medium of feeling, through feeling that you are already what you want to be. And that is how you grow exceedingly great in your world, for you will be the Jacob expanding in your world.

The next one we come upon is Job. Here in the midst of all the trials and tribulations of a man, Job says, "I will hold fast to my righteousness and then my heart shall never judge me harshly as long as I live." He will hold fast to righteousness in the midst of storm, in the midst of all the problems of the world he will assume that he is free and hold fast to that right consciousness knowing that not in eternity could his heart ever judge him harshly.

Then we are told, "The meek of the earth seek righteousness and it is to the meek of the earth that the earth is given. As you are told the meek shall inherit the earth. You might have been taught to believe it meant the beaten man, the man who falls and grovels like the grasshopper; it doesn't. The word "meek" if translated actually means to be tamed as a wild animal is tamed. To the man who tames the mind, the man who tames his being that he can set it any task and have it execute that task, that man is meek and the meek inherit the earth. And the meek always seek righteousness, so if I today began to subdue this earth, I must make righteousness my watchword, and so if I were righteous I would now single out the nature of the trees I would plant, the nature of the flowers I would plant, the nature of the animals I would cultivate, the nature of the fish that I would catch, and I would name them as desirable states, called in the Bible beauty instead of ashes, called in the Bible the spirit of joy instead of mourning, called by all these lovely things. As you are told, all the things that are good, dwell on these things. To every good thing, for He called it very good. Everything that I would call the good, which is a righteous judgment, will be the right judgment. I, in spite of the evidence of my senses that would deny it, in spite of reason that would tell me that it was impossible of realization, having discovered that I am the one planting my garden, that this is the only garden to cultivate, that this is the only earth to subdue, I would start now and boldly assume the good, first for myself -always start with Jerusalem -then go into the world and preach the goodness by knowing the goodness.

When you meet someone, regardless of what the appearance would reveal, know the truth for that one and set him free. Know that knowing as he ought to be known first by himself, but if he hasn't known it as true of himself, you at least know it for him. And though you never meet him in the flesh again keep on knowing the truth that sets man free by knowing he is already free, and you are cultivating your garden. You are bringing it into subjection, you are subduing it and then you shall have dominion. So you are supreme in your world if you only know the world that you really are; so man is the psychological earth on which this wonderful whirl of events takes place. Man is the psychological earth on which all the animals move; every emotion is symbolized as the animal. Every fowl of the air is truly the idea you entertain. Every fish of the deep is the invisible state that you could catch if you only knew how to cast your net on the right side. For you fish all night and catch nothing, but then comes one who knows, who is righteous, and he casts it on the right side, always that right side, and the right side is righteousness or right consciousness. And I will catch it; I may not see them, I don't have to see them. I don't have to wait for the evidence of my senses to confirm, for I am told, "And faith was accounted unto him for righteousness." So I will have faith in the reality of the deep; I will have faith in the reality of invisible states. So it's now invisible, I know it, it's a fish, but I have faith in the existence and the reality of the invisible state I want to externalize, knowing I can externalize it, for every time I externalize it I add to this wonderful garment of my Father, and that is my job, my duty.

So here, every one of us, begin to believe that you are the only earth spoken of in the Bible. You are the one chosen to live in the center of the garden, but make it a garden, for the words are, "Keep it, keep it and plant it well". You have dominion over every idea in your mind. You say you haven't. Well, some may be to you disturbing, but you do have the choice of rejecting it or accepting it.

If you accept it, you identify with it and the state with which you are identified must, by the very law of your being, objectify itself within your world, that you may see by it how you plant that garden. Now, don't wait one second beyond the time that you observe weeds instead of flowers. Start right at the moment of observation, and start to replant the garden. Start really to subdue it. Become the meek and the meek is the bold. The meek is the bold of heart who does not ask assistance. He walks knowing he can do it. He can fish. He can actually bring into subjection every bird of the air, every idea of the mind. He will begin to know these things spiritually. He will know them in the only way that you and I should know anything, by becoming it, not to have a world of information concerning objective things, and knowing these things only mentally. I must learn to know things spiritually; I must learn to know what love is spiritually by being in love. I must learn to know what security is spiritually be becoming conscious of already being secure. I must learn to know what health is by becoming conscious of already being healthy, and sustain these states in the name of righteousness, knowing that my righteousness shall answer for me in time to come.

Make me no promise for when the father-in-law said to Jacob, "What promise should I make you?" "Just tell me that the offspring born in a certain manner shall be mine and no other promise, and no wages and no salary, all the spotted ones are mine. There isn't a spotted one among the parents but every offspring that is spotted, though the parents are not, that is mine. That's my wage and my righteousness shall know it for me in time to come." And he begins to assume that his world is peopled with the spotted calves, and everyone born that was healthy was born spotted. And he increased beyond the wildest dream of a man.

Well, become that man, and start from the simple beginning as he started. There wasn't one thing in the world to encourage him that one calf could ever be born from parents that were not spotted and be a spotted calf. Yet he knew and he assumed that they had given birth to such things in numbers, they would come and they came a thousand fold. So in your case, maybe it's business, maybe the doctors have given you a final, final verdict and it's fatal. Well, I say in spite of this, and the doctor in his own way is doing his best, he would not have said it to hurt you or to frighten you. He firmly believed it, but you have another law and your law is that you can assume, in spite of that verdict, that you are well. And then, though tomorrow and the next day the tree doesn't appear, know that in time your righteousness shall speak for you, and like Job in the midst of all the storms, when he should have gone to the grave, he held fast to the consciousness of already being what he wanted to be, that his heart may not in time speak harshly against him. Well, it didn't -you know the story.

And so, all through we are told, "Break off the sins, break off missing marks by righteousness. Blessed are they that hunger and thirst after righteousness, for they shall be filled."

Now you are told, "Seek first the kingdom of God and His righteousness and all things shall be added unto you." Well, the kingdom of God is within you. You have been told that a number of times. The Bible affirms it over and over -"The Kingdom of God and the kingdom of heaven are within you." They aren't without. You see them seemingly without; that is the response to the within-ness where they are. Now, seek it and His righteousness. So assume within the mood that would be yours were you already the man that you want to be. Sustain that mood, occupy it as often as you can, and see how that righteousness shall draw things unto itself, and the things it draws are always in harmony with its nature. It never draws anything foreign to itself. If I assume that I am the man I want to be, I cannot then encounter events that are in conflict with my assumption. For my world mirrors the being I am.

So, here, today when you return read the whole chapter. It's beautiful. But I started with the 27th verse, "And God made man in his own image, in the image of God made He him. Male and female made He them." Then comes what is to be done. Then comes the promise if you do it. Then comes the judgment, "It is good and very good." So you start knowing that you are the earth on which you now start to labor. If you do it, you shall be fruitful, and you will multiply, and you actually replenish this world, though it seemingly is barren you replenish it, if you subdue it. And the earth is self to be subdued, not by beating self as some people have misunderstood, not by isolating the self in some little secluded spot, not by running away from life, but in the midst of life is the opportunity to become meek: to take the violence that is man, it is individual man, and then bring it into the state of the meek, to transcend the violence by not fighting against conditions; know that conditions can only reflect what is within the one who observes that condition. So don't rage against it; leave it just as it is. If conditions remain the same, that is a sure, sure sign that you have not been faithful to righteousness.

Had you been faithful to the consciousness of already being the man you want to be, conditions would have to change in harmony with that righteousness. So don't rage against it; leave it as it is, and start today to take this wonderful earth, which is the foot stool of the Lord, which really is the mind of man, and start really to work upon it. Then you will not turn from left to right; you will keep the narrow path. You will go out knowing you can do it.

I know from experience it will not take long to see shoots appear; it will not take long to see the flowers appear. They will all appear, if you will take yourself in hand and by an uncritical observation of self watch the being you are; see the condition of the earth as it is now by the uncritical observation of your reactions to life. When you see who you are that is showing you the state of the earth as it is now. Don't condemn it, just start to subdue it, and know that you do have dominion over all the fish of the sea, the fowls of the air, and all the animals that move upon the earth. Knowing them to be the moods of thought, the desires, the passions that move in you, start to entertain only the good and the very good.

Dwell upon them and you will re-people your earth for you are supreme within the circle of your own consciousness. Now you may say it's a very little one; may I tell you that though you have a body and a life of your own, you are rooted in me, and you end in me, as I am rooted in God and end in God.

So every man can say the same thing no matter if you look into a world of 2,500,000,000 of them and every year they slip through the gates into the invisible state relative to this world, but as they come and go every man in the world is actually rooted in you and ends in you, and you are rooted in the ultimate that we call God, the Father. So the whole vast (world) is simply centered in you; start now to rearrange it that it may reflect the beauty that you want to live about and live in in this world. You do it by assuming the best. Always imagine the best of self; always imagine first with Jerusalem and then go out and radiate what you have given to self. If you live in that wonderful state yourself, you will only have the good to shower upon others, for you have one gift that is truly yours to give and that is yourself. You have no other gift. If you are good, you can give only the good. If you are not -well, whatever you are -that you give.

So the story is you may find today when you observe yourself, by observing your reactions, that it's not a very pleasant land but it is still a fertile land; it can be cleared of all these trees of traditional wrong thinking and can be replanted in harmony with the beauty that you desire. And in the immediate present it will bear fruit in harmony with the seeds you plant.

So let us go out determined to bring about a better arrangement of our mind that we may produce more noble garments for our Father to wear. For this wonderful, visible, objective universe is only the living garment of my Father, it's not a place of exile, as so many believe, talking about home and their going home, as though they are not now in the very midst of their Father. When you see me, you see my Father. Whenever you see me, you see the state of my mind, for you will see the world in which I live and the state of my mind, that inner arrangement, that's my Father. When you see me projected, you then call it the Son, and my world round about me tells me where I am. All these inner states are places in this fabulous psychological consciousness. Inner state is equal to place and where I stand within myself determines what I see when I look outside the self. So, when I look out upon the world, that area of my Father's garment, whether it be torn by reason of the inner place where I stand or whether it be lovely, I see only the inner arrangement of myself. I am forever surrounding myself with the true image of myself, and what I am in consciousness that only can I see. Knowing that, let me be determined today to seek righteousness, or right consciousness, that I may reap in the immediate present all the lovely things that I desire.

Now in summary, single out some noble aim in life. Having defined it clearly to yourself as a desirable state. the state you would like to externalize, ask yourself this very simple question, "What would the feeling be like were it true if I already embodied that noble state?" In response to your question will come a feeling; assume that feeling; it has reality outside of the present moment. Its being is in complete independence of present objective fact. It has real structure; it has reality in the deep of it. It came in response to your call when you said, "What would the feeling be like were it true?" And you named what you were thinking of -if it was security, if it was health, if it was any state, that fish came from the deep; it's located and you took the "I" and placed it in that feeling. You were actually standing upon it though it is invisible. Now remain on it.

If you remain in that state, you are told in the Bible three days, you will be "spewed out on dry land." "Three" doesn't mean three days; "three" means fullness, "three" means complete. So if I will live within that fish for three days until the whole thing seems natural and seems real, and it has the sensory vividness of reality. I will then be spewed out as something objective, and something that is commonly called in the Bible "land" or "dry land." But it does have reality, as you feel it, only people get away from it because it doesn't have immediate objective fact to confirm it. But you ride it for your three days and you will know what it was to enter that fish and remain in it until fullness was attained, until reality was attained within. In that state you were righteous and your righteousness will speak for you in time to come. It will not fail you; it cannot fail you.

Lightning Source UK Ltd.
Milton Keynes UK
UKOW042011210513

211049UK00001B/284/P